Sometimes the Profoundest Truths Are Best Illuminated through Simple Stories

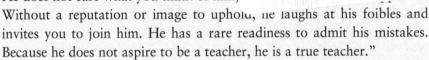

"The Mulla is happy to break convention... He does not care what you think of him; ... ... Without a reputation or image to uphold, he laughs at his foibles and invites you to join him. He has a rare readiness to admit his mistakes. Because he does not aspire to be a teacher, he is a true teacher."

—FROM THE INTRODUCTION

Sufi teachers know that humor is an especially effective teaching tool, for laughter opens our hearts so that insights are able to penetrate more deeply. From this truth emerged the mythical Mulla Nasruddin. A Muslim of Middle Eastern origin but with universal insights that make him a citizen of the world, the Mulla's wisdom stories address the bewildering and hilarious mysteries that seekers of all traditions encounter in our spiritual lives.

Whether the Mulla is carrying his donkey through the marketplace, explaining the pregnancy of a cooking pot to a neighbor, or rescuing the moon from the bottom of a well, his comic teaching tales remind us that we all carry the sacred within—whether we call it Allah, Jesus, Elohim, Krishna, or any other name—and we are foolish not to realize and work toward our astounding potential.

Also Available

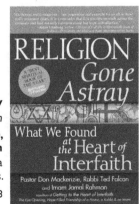

IMAM JAMAL RAHMAN is a beloved teacher and retreat leader whose passion for helping people deepen their spiritual lives and cultivate interfaith understanding has inspired audiences throughout the world. He has been featured in the *New York Times*, on *CBS News*, the BBC and many NPR programs. He is co-founder and Muslim Sufi minister at Interfaith Community Sanctuary, adjunct faculty at Seattle University, and a former host of Interfaith Talk Radio. He is author of *Spiritual Gems of Islam: Insights & Practices from the Qur'an, Hadith, Rumi & Muslim Teaching Stories to Enlighten the Heart & Mind* (SkyLight Paths) and *The Fragrance of Faith: The Enlightened Heart of Islam;* and co-author of *Getting to the Heart of Interfaith: The Eye-Opening, Hope-Filled Friendship of a Pastor, a Rabbi & an Imam* and *Religion Gone Astray: What We Found at the Heart of Interfaith* (both SkyLight Paths), among other books.

"Marvelous…. Lasers into the heart of the matter with delicious humor. Truly a lovely book for people of all faith traditions."
—**KAY LINDAHL**, co-founder, Women of Spirit and Faith; co-editor, *Women, Spirituality and Transformative Leadership: Where Grace Meets Power*

"There are many books on Sufism, but none like this! The wisdom presented here, made all the more sharp by the liberating humor that carries it, is a scalpel cutting away everything that distracts us from Truth."
—**RABBI RAMI SHAPIRO**, author, *Perennial Wisdom for the Spiritually Independent: Sacred Teachings—Annotated and Explained*

"In case you were tempted to characterize Islam as dogmatic or somber, [here is] the Mulla, and his most eloquent spokesperson, Imam Jamal Rahman. Be prepared to laugh your head off and then … have a direct and transformational encounter with the wild wisdom of the Sufis."
—**MIRABAI STARR**, author, *God of Love: A Guide to the Heart of Judaism, Christianity and Islam*

Also Available from Imam Jamal Rahman

Spiritual Gems of Islam
Insights & Practices from the Qur'an, Hadith, Rumi & Muslim Teaching Stories to Enlighten the Heart & Mind
By Imam Jamal Rahman
This practical guide for spiritual seekers of all traditions shows how the gems of Islamic spirituality can help you increase your capacity for joy, sorrow, compassion and wonder.
6 x 9, 256 pp, Quality PB Original, 978-1-59473-430-4

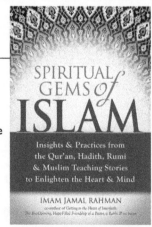

SPIRITUAL*/* GEMS *of* ISLAM
Insights & Practices from the Qur'an, Hadith, Rumi & Muslim Teaching Stories to Enlighten the Heart & Mind

IMAM JAMAL RAHMAN

SACRED
Laughter
OF THE
Sufis

Awakening the Soul with the
Mulla's Comic Teaching Stories
& Other Islamic Wisdom

IMAM JAMAL RAHMAN

Walking Together, Finding the Way®

SKYLIGHT PATHS®
PUBLISHING

Sacred Laughter of the Sufis:
Awakening the Soul with the Mulla's Comic Teaching Stories & Other
Islamic Wisdom

2014 Quality Paperback Edition, First Printing
© 2014 by Jamal Rahman

Library of Congress Cataloging-in-Publication Data
Rahman, Jamal.
  Sacred laughter of the Sufis : awakening the soul with the mulla's comic teaching stories & other Islamic wisdom / Imam Jamal Rahman.
     pages cm
  Includes bibliographical references and index.
  ISBN 978-1-59473-547-9 (quality pbk. : alk. paper) — ISBN 978-1-59473-564-6 (ebook : alk. paper) 1. Sufi parables. 2. Sufi parables—History and criticism. 3. Sufism—Doctrines. I. Title.
  BP189.63.R34 2014
  297.4'382—dc23
                                        2014004046

Manufactured in United States of America

Cover Design: Jenny Buono
Interior Design: Michael Myers

SkyLight Paths Publishing is creating a place where people of different spiritual traditions come together for challenge and inspiration, a place where we can help each other understand the mystery that lies at the heart of our existence.

SkyLight Paths sees both believers and seekers as a community that increasingly transcends traditional boundaries of religion and denomination—people want-ing to learn from each other, *walking together, finding the way.*

Walking Together, Finding the Way
Published by SkyLight Paths Publishing
www.skylightpaths.com

ISBN 978-1-68336-274-6 (hc)

Contents

BE ENGAGED IN THE WORLD

TIME TO RETURN HOME

Introduction

This book is about spiritual insights conveyed through teaching stories and sacred verses or poetry. The profoundest truth is sometimes best expressed through a simple story or an illuminating verse. The ancients say that a precious gold coin is often recovered with the help of a penny candle.

Sufi teachers make prolific use of the technique of combining stories and relevant verses (from the Qur'an, sayings of the Prophet Muhammad, and sacred poetry) and asking the student to meditate on them. Hopefully a fresh insight will emerge. *Hal* in Sufism is a condition, mood, or receptivity in one's being that stems from an insight that arises in the heart. *Maqam* is a station attained by the continuous process of reflecting on and living the higher awareness gained by the insight. Through this experiential process, something shifts within and one evolves into a higher station. Sufi teachers describe the higher station as follows: "Once the blush of the Beloved graces you, there is no going back to becoming a green apple."

My hope in compiling this collection of stories and insights is that they will touch your heart with new insights of your own and inspire you to *live* those insights as you evolve spiritually into your higher self.

Sufi teachers know that humor is an especially effective teaching tool, for laughter opens our heart so that insights are able to penetrate more deeply. "If you want special illumination," says the thirteenth-century mystic Rumi, "look upon the human face; see clearly within laughter, the essence of ultimate truth." And the fourteenth-century sage Hafiz wrote, "What is this precious love and laughter budding in our hearts? Listen ... It is the glorious sound of a soul waking up!" Of all the spiritual practices taught to me by my Sufi parents and other teachers, the most beneficial was the gift of laughter, thanks to these humorous teaching stories. The stories and verses in this book are my personal favorites. They have continued to yield their insights over many years of retelling and meditation.

The Sufis: Spirituality over Law

In general, Sufis are Muslims who prefer essence over form. A great majority of Sufis follow the same tenets of Islam as other Muslims do, but focus more on the spirit than on the letter of the law. Thus if they don't manage to perform the five obligatory prayers every day, they make up for it by performing acts of charity or some other service. After all, the Holy Qur'an almost always presents a verse on service following a verse on prayer. Sufis are accused by conservative Muslims of being overly flexible, but Sufis smilingly reply, "Blessed are the flexible for they will never be bent out of shape!"

Sufism emerged at a time when seventh-century Islam was experiencing exponential growth and becoming a global empire. A growing number of people who called themselves Sufis were alarmed that the spirituality of Islam was being sullied and overshadowed by the needs of empire building. As early as the eighth century, commenting on the unholy alliance of powerful rulers, religious institutions, and clerics, a spiritual teacher named Hasan of Basra said that real Islam was in the books and real Muslims were in the tomb.[1] In contemporary times, when Muslim countries are beset by problems of economic deprivation and political violence, Sufis and other Muslims continue to struggle to preserve the spiritual teachings of Islam.

It is important to note that Sufism is not a denomination of Islam. The two main denominations are Sunni (85 percent) and Shia (15 percent); their differences can be traced to a dispute about the choice of a community leader after the death of the Prophet Muhammad in 632 CE. Both denominations share the same teachings of Islam, but the historical conflict created emotional wounds that have been slow to heal, and the small theological differences between the two groups are often exploited by the unscrupulous for economic and political advantage.

There are both Sunni and Shia Sufis. In fact, there are also non-Muslim Sufis, primarily Christians, Jews, Buddhists, and Hindus who practice Sufi spirituality and call themselves Sufis. How is this "dual citizenship" possible? Sufis explain this with a metaphor. During prayer, Muslims bow and prostrate themselves in the direction of the symbolic house of God, the Kabah in Mecca. What happens if non-Muslims, following their chosen path, become enlightened? It is as if they are praying *inside* the Kabah. In that state, does it matter in what direction the prayer rug is pointing?

Mulla Nasruddin and His Philosophy

There are, of course, different kinds of Sufis, and some are more liberal than others. But overall, Sufis have one thing in common: They laugh a lot! Over the centuries, from this sustained laughter has emerged the mythical Mulla Nasruddin. The Mulla agrees with Sufi teachers that there is much to laugh about in the bewildering and hilarious mysteries that we encounter in our spiritual lives. For example:

- If God wanted, He could have sent full-blown enlightened beings to Earth, but He chose to send imperfect beings like us.
- How astonishing that God hides from humanity, creating wild speculations and crazy strife. As Rumi exclaims, "The lover visible, the Beloved invisible: whose crazy idea was this?"
- All traditions that mention God proclaim that Divinity is genderless, yet the holy books and practitioners insist on calling God by a masculine pronoun.
- No human being who has arrived here from the mysterious realms has ever come with a mandate or mission statement, yet some of us talk and argue as if we know why we are here, and others talk as if they don't care.
- None of our revealed holy books has ever been accompanied by footnotes, yet we argue as if we know the real meanings.
- We are all afraid that one day we shall pass away into nonexistence. But if the truth be known, nonexistence is trembling in fear that it might be given human shape.
- When we go over to the other side and look back at our dramas and melodramas, we shall laugh and laugh. So why don't we laugh right now?

The Mulla is a village idiot and sage rolled into one. Although he has no formal education, he wears a turban, signaling that he is a person of learning. His wisdom appears to emanate from a source beyond book learning. The most popular image of the Mulla is the picture of him riding backward on his donkey, sometimes followed by adoring students. In this picture, many metaphors abound. The Mulla has tamed his donkey ego—it knows in which direction to go. The Mulla does not believe in hierarchy and faults religious institutions and clerics for their rigidity and lust for glory and power. Rather than turn his back on students, he prefers to face them. Most of all, he is happy to break conventional patterns of thinking and being. The Mulla does not care what you think of him; he does not seek your approval. Without a reputation or image to uphold, he laughs at his foibles and invites you to join him. He has a rare readiness to admit his mistakes. Because he does not aspire to be a teacher, he is a true teacher.

The Mulla is timeless and placeless. The earliest written accounts of him appeared in the thirteenth century and there is mention of him meeting Jelaluddin Rumi, but oral stories of him were being told as early as the eighth century. He is a Muslim of Middle Eastern origin, but because his insights are universal, he is accepted as a citizen of the world. The Mulla is a popular figure, for example, in contemporary China.

Most of the Mulla stories are fictional but are rooted in metaphors and images of the Qur'an and sayings of the Prophet Muhammad. The Prophet asks us to go as far as China in search of knowledge, and, sure enough, the Mulla travels to that country. The Holy Book mentions ships, storms, stars, and the Moon, and the Mulla is often a ferry captain, navigating storms, rescuing the Moon from a well, and talking about how old Moons are scissored by God to become stars. Some stories are based on historical incidents. A Mulla story parallels a famous meeting between the fourteenth-century poet Hafiz and the most feared conqueror of his time, Timurlane. After sweeping through Persia, Timurlane summoned the aging Hafiz to answer for the offense of writing a few lines about offering Bokhara, the conqueror's native town, in exchange for the mole on a girl's cheek. "You're right," replied Hafiz bowing quickly. "It's by just such extravagant spending that I've come to the sorry position you find me in now." Timurlane was so pleased by Hafiz's quick-thinking wit that he spared his life and sent him away with a gift, an outcome repeated in the Mulla story.

The Mulla stories convey a common thread of Sufi teachings, which can be summarized as follows:

- Every human has a divine spark veiled by the layers of personality. Whether we call it Allah, Jesus, Elohim, Krishna, or any other name, that spark is the same and we are foolish not to realize our astounding potential.

- An essential spiritual practice is to observe and witness oneself continuously and compassionately, acknowledging and laughing at foibles and weaknesses while working relentlessly to evolve into higher consciousness.
- The light of persistent awareness is bound, little by little, to dissolve our false self and bring us closer to our authentic self. We may not become perfect human beings, but that is not the goal. The goal is to become more aligned with our higher self and expand our worldview as we learn to see the Face of God in everyone we meet.
- Institutions and those who serve institutions cannot be trusted to acknowledge their weaknesses and serve the common good, and we would be wise to emulate the Mulla's healthy skepticism about their moral leadership.
- Our human understanding of divine verses, such as those in the Qur'an, can be less than divine.
- With grace and courage we must work to change or eliminate religious customs and scriptural interpretations that do not meet the test of divine compassion and generosity.

This Spiritual Journey: Identity through Accountability

This book consists of forty-eight brief chapters running the gamut from our first spiritual inclinations to the completion of our spiritual journey. The section called "Our Human Condition" describes the search for our true identity. "Some Shifts in Awareness" delves into how crises in life cause us to ask deeper questions. In "Foibles and Vulnerabilities" we probe our longing for approval from others, our slavish dependence on experts, our hearty appetite for praise and titles, and our attachment to the familiar. "Wariness of Religious Institutions" examines the corruption of these institutions as a result of deferred spiritual maintenance, defunct religious customs, and faith in borrowed certainty. "Spiritual Practices" focuses on honoring the present moment, practicing gratitude, and engaging in prayers and rituals, among others. "Wisdom for the Inner Journey" offers timeless wisdom from spiritual sages to help us on our inner path. Topics include the art of searching in the right direction, doing the work little by little and with a sense of balance, connecting to authentic teachers, understanding the mysterious web of interconnectedness, and learning to celebrate diversity. "Knowing God" examines what it means to connect with Mystery. "Be Engaged in the World" explores doing what is beautiful, building community, pursuing justice, and honoring women and children. And, finally, "Time to Return Home" reminds us that, sooner or later, we shall return to our Source and be asked to account for how we have lived our lives. (Take heart; the afterlife is not necessarily what we think it is.)

How to Use This Book

Each chapter is self-contained, consisting of stories and insights followed by reflections and practices. The reflections include relevant Qur'anic verses, sayings of the Prophet Muhammad, and sacred poetry or sayings of Islamic (usually Sufi) sages. A handful of chapters also include insights and poetry from Hindu and Buddhist sources. Practices consist of questions to stimulate self-reflection, sometimes followed by at least one spiritual exercise.

You may want to start the book from the beginning, but since each small chapter is independent, you may start from any point. What is useful is to linger with the stories and verses that feel relevant to you. Allow them to resonate and percolate in you.

Choose questions and practices that appeal to you. Mull over the questions and give yourself time to experience the spiritual techniques. Most important of all, give yourself permission to laugh. You will receive the blessings of the Mulla!

Sources for Qur'an, *Hadith*, and Islamic Poets

Qur'anic translations are primarily from *The Meaning of the Holy Qur'an,* translated by Yusuf Ali. Other translations are from *The Message of the Qur'an* by Muhammad Asad and *The Light of Dawn: Daily Readings from the Holy Qur'an* by Camille Helminski. These books are listed in Suggestions for Further Reading.

Many scholars have collected sayings of the Prophet Muhammad (called *hadith* in Arabic). *Hadith* are the Prophet's own words, and *hadith qudsi* are God's words communicated to the Prophet, usually through a dream. Since all these collections are based on hearsay, it is hard to verify which ones are genuine. According to many Islamic scholars, there are six scholars, all from the ninth century, whose collections are considered more authentic than others. These collections are as follows:

> *Sahih al-Bukhari,* collected by Imam Bukhari (d. 870)
>
> *Sahih Muslim,* collected by Imam Muslim (d. 875)
>
> *Sunan an-Nasa'i,* collected by Imam Nasa'i (d. 915)
>
> *Sunnan Abu Dawud,* collected by Imam Abu Dawud (d. 888)
>
> *Sunnan al-Tirmidhi,* collected by Imam Tirmidhi (d. 892)
>
> *Sunnan Ibn Maja,* collected by Imam Ibn Maja (d. 886)

Most of the *hadith* quoted in this book come from one of the six authentic collections listed above and are not individually cited. Only when a *hadith* is drawn from outside of these collections is attribution included in the text.

Besides Qur'anic verses and *hadith,* I have included brief utterances by the thirteenth-century sage Rumi. These are based on translations by Kabir and Camille Helminski and by Coleman Barks. The books I have used are listed below:

> *Jewels of Remembrance: A Daybook of Spiritual Guidance Containing 365 Selections from the Wisdom of Rumi,* by Camille and Kabir Helminski
>
> *Rumi: Daylight—A Daybook of Spiritual Guidance,* by Camille and Kabir Helminski
>
> *The Essential Rumi,* by Coleman Barks

In a few instances I used sayings from the fourteenth-century poet Hafiz. The translations are by Daniel Ladinsky from his books titled *The Gift* and *Love Poems to God.* A complete listing of these books is found in Suggestions for Further Reading.

Traditional Sufi sayings that appear without attribution are the gifts of oral transmission from my parents, who heard them from their parents and grandparents going back many generations.

Our Human
Condition

Searching for Our True Identity

A stranger seeking to meet Bayazid Bistami, a ninth-century Sufi sage, came to his door and said, "I'm looking for Bayazid." The master replied, "The truth is that I myself have been looking for him for the last thirty years."

What was true of Bistami is true of us as well: We humans are searching for our authentic selves all our lives. Whether our egos acknowledge it or not, our souls know that an essential purpose of life is to identify and manifest the unique spark of Divinity at the core of our being. Sadly, too often we seek identity through titles, awards, and riches, and though we may gain those earthly rewards, we don't find what we are really looking for. As the days of our lives begin to run out, we waste them in frenetic activity, never stopping to hear the Qur'an's poignant question, "Where are you going?" We are like the Mulla, seated on his donkey and rushing through the marketplace. Friends hail him and want to chat, but he replies, "Not now. Can't you see I'm busy? I'm looking for my donkey!"

That simple Mulla story captures the predicament of the human journey, and it is worth our while to explore the many facets of its teachings. One message is that it is critical to slow down. Whether our haste is driven by needs of survival or longing for glory, our souls need to experience moments of quiet time. Ours is a world of noise, distractions, conflict, and bewilderment. In quiet moments, our beings are refreshed, hope springs alive, and love blossoms.

Equally important is the need to pay attention to friends who hail us in the marketplace. The cycle of life is completed faster than we think. Enjoy the sweet joys of life that family, friends, and this world offer. The Qur'an says that God, out of love for humanity, has made his bounties flow to you "in exceeding measure, seen and unseen" (31:20), so it is a valid spiritual practice to "enjoy the beautiful things of life."

Another important message is that in the journey to find our true selves, we must first become conscious of the search and of ourselves as seekers. If we rush heedlessly like the Mulla on his donkey, we will get discouraged and frustrated. But if we slow down and allow ourselves to be spiritual seekers, not demanding a certain outcome, we will learn the wisdom of an age-old insight: "That which we speak of can never be found by seeking, yet only seekers find."[1]

Sooner or later, true seekers awaken to the most essential message: We cannot find our true identity by looking outside of ourselves. If we define ourselves solely by our profession, material success or failure, or personal status, we have simply described our ego, and we can never satisfy the needs of the ego. The ego is like the donkey in the Mulla story, carrying us hither and yon without a clue about what we are truly looking for. Mysteriously nestled inside of us, beyond our ego, is the divine spark, our higher self, our true identity. Call it the spark of Allah, Elohim, Jesus, Buddha, Krishna, or our essential humanity. Once we awaken to that higher self, we become what religions variously describe as "freed," "surrendered," or "saved." We are released from slavery to our personal "donkey" and discover the joy of riding a "donkey with wings," as Islamic spirituality describes the transformed ego.

That delightful metaphor is derived from the Prophet's account of a glorious night flight on a winged steed, which miraculously transported him from Mecca to Jerusalem, where he ascended upward into the realms of Mystery. On the basis of the Prophet's descriptions of that mysterious event, known as the *miraj*, Islamic tradition depicts the Prophet mounted on a donkeylike creature with wings. Thus the lowly donkey can be transformed into a steed that will carry us beyond the earthly limits of our human ego, even into spiritual ecstasy.

But can our donkey egos really sprout wings? Consider the story of Mahatma Gandhi, who was physically removed from a train cabin and thrown to the platform one cold night because he had dared to sit with South African whites. Seething with anger and resentment, his bruised ego sought revenge. But Gandhi knew instinctively that this was not his true identity speaking, nor was it his true calling to seek retaliation. He sought to connect with his higher self and choose a higher path. He deepened his inner spiritual practices and restrained the reactions of his ego. After several years, he humbly declared that he would like to make one boast if allowed: He could no longer feel any anger or hate against any oppressor or enemy, no matter how unjust or cruel that person's behavior might be. Deep inside, he was able to flower into higher consciousness—and that, he said, is something that every human can do. We all have a higher identity, and we are all capable of finding and expressing it.

 # REFLECTIONS

The human being was born restless (Qur'an 70:19), but truly in the remembrance of God do hearts find rest. (Qur'an 13:28)

You are the traveler; you are the path; you are the destination. Be careful never to lose the way to yourself.[2] (Yahya Suhrawardi)

Give up these ten days of famousness and revolve with me around the Sun that never sets. (Rumi)

 # PRACTICE

At this time, how do you evaluate yourself and others? What benchmarks do you use for defining personal success or failure?

Make a list of qualities of being that you consider high ideals, and that you would most like to cultivate in yourself. Now list ego attributes that hold you back, and that you would like to minimize in your life. Express gratitude for the awareness of the difference between divine qualities and ego attributes.

Create an appropriate affirmation, self-talk, or prayer about your divine self, using language that is aligned with your belief system. For example, "Every day in every way, my personality is becoming more and more aligned with my higher self."

Stuck in Patterns

If there is one word to describe a common human predicament, that word is *stuck*. We are stuck, individually and collectively, in unhelpful patterns of thinking and being, which we repeat unconsciously while becoming ever more frustrated and unhappy. Loudly, we bemoan our lot and find something or someone to blame, seldom realizing that we ourselves are the cause of our repetitious patterns and that we have the power to break them. We are like the Mulla who complained every day at lunch that he was getting sick and tired of cheese sandwiches. His coworkers listened to his complaints for several days, and finally they offered him some advice. "Mulla, tell your wife to make you something different. Be persuasive with her." "But I'm not married," replied the Mulla. "Well, then," they asked, "who makes your lunch?" "I do!" replied the Mulla.

Some years ago we had a series of meetings in our house of worship about what we could do at grassroots levels about the selfish greed of megacorporations and financial institutions. It dawned on us that we the complainers were also the supporters and sustainers of these institutions. We shopped and banked with the cartels and their subsidiaries we condemned. Until we ourselves changed our personal habits, how could we expect changes on a larger level? It was the same story when we examined our disapproval of media monopolies and their focus on sensationalism. As their consumers, we support and sustain them.

In my classes when I bring up this particular Mulla story and ask for examples, medical practitioners and people with multiple divorces are quick to raise their hands. The former recognize this phenomenon in some patients who lament their deteriorating medical conditions and blame their illness on genes and destiny. Because change is inconvenient, they underplay and often ignore the critical need to change their lifestyle and diet, both of which could radically change the course of their disease. The latter, some of whom have remarried as many as four times and have complained bitterly about their partners, recognize that they have been stuck in the pattern of remarrying the same person, different in name and time, but similar in dysfunctional behavior.

Our life path is metaphorically strewn with rocks and thorns, said the twenty-century Hindu sage Ramama Maharshi, and we waste enormous time and energy whining and rolling out carpets to cushion our tender toes. Instead, he asked, "Why don't you simply wear sturdier sandals or shoes?"

REFLECTION

We learn from history that we do not learn from history. (Traditional Sufi saying, which in the West is attributed to Friedrich Hegel.)

PRACTICE

What is one "cheese sandwich" pattern in your life? Choose a simple but effective change that you could make to alter this pattern. Try it for a week. Do you notice any positive shifts?

Find a friend whom you trust. Share your pattern with him, inviting him to also share with you. Throughout the week, check in with each other. How are you both progressing in adjusting your behaviors? Having a support system while making major life shifts is crucial.

Overlooking the Obvious

A traveler approached the Mulla, who was working in his garden, and asked in which direction he should walk to reach a certain town. The Mulla pointed the way, and when the man asked how long it would take him to reach his destination, the Mulla stared at him and resumed his gardening. The man asked again, but the Mulla ignored him. Cursing the Mulla, the man started to walk. After a little while, the Mulla shouted out, "Three hours!" When the man angrily asked why he hadn't answered earlier, the Mulla replied, "First I had to see how fast you walk."

The subtle humor of this story lies in the idea that something so obvious is so easily overlooked. Without the proper direction, we are lost; without a steady commitment to the journey, we slacken and go astray. Upon reflection it would appear that our primary purpose in life is to evolve into the fullness of our being. The Qur'an declares that each of us was created not for "idle sport" but for a "just cause" and a "determined time." All our actions and acquisitions, precious though they may be to us, are secondary to our sacred and foremost duty to move in the direction of realizing our "just cause" and sacred potential.

Sufi teachers are insistent on this point, and Rumi is particularly passionate about it. In the Masnavi, Rumi's extensive poem of spiritual and ethical teachings, he says that if we perform and remember everything else, yet forget our essential purpose, then we have done nothing whatsoever. All things are assigned a task, Rumi says: The Heavens send rain and light to the Earth; the Earth brings forth blossoms and fruits; the mountains offer mines of gold and silver. As for the human task, Rumi invokes the Qur'an: "Truly, We offered the trust to the Heavens, and to the Earth, and to the mountains; but they refused to undertake it"—that is, they were happy enough just to be Heavens, Earth, and mountains without responsibility or choice in the matter—"but the human being undertook it, though he was indeed unjust and foolish" (33:72). In other words, primordial humans accepted the "trust" of free will in the matter of achieving our divine purpose, but we are often foolish and behave in ways that betray and belie our higher being. We ignore the sacred trust. Again, Rumi invokes metaphors to lament our unconscious choices. Our God-given potential is like a golden pot worth hundreds of ordinary pots, he says, but we use it to boil ragged turnips. Or it is like a gem-studded Damascene sword, but we use it as a peg to hang a lowly gourd. Why not use the golden pot to boil the dross of our ego and wield the heavenly sword to cleave through the ego's veils of arrogance and ignorance?

How urgent and necessary is our inner work? Let's hear it from the Mulla, who, as a ferry captain, met a famous scholar of religion on a four-day journey aboard his ferry. On the first night, the scholar asked the Mulla if had read the Qur'an in Arabic. No, said the Mulla, he had never learned Arabic. "How unfortunate," lamented the professor. "Without a foundation in Arabic, you have missed out on the subtleties of the Holy Book. I am afraid that you have wasted half your life." The next night, he asked the Mulla if he had heard of famous Islamic sages such as Rumi, Hafiz, or Ibn Arabi. No, the Mulla knew very little about them. "How incredible!" commented the scholar. "Truly, you have wasted three-fourths of your life." The third night, a fierce storm arose. The Mulla rushed to the scholar's cabin and shouted, "Professor, do you know something about swimology?" The scholar asked if the Mulla meant something to do with swimming. "Yes! Yes!" exclaimed the Mulla. "Oh, in my busy life I never had time to learn how to swim," replied the scholar. "How tragic!" sighed the Mulla. "The ferry is sinking and we have no lifeboats or life jackets. I am so sorry to tell you that you have wasted all your life!"

The Mulla story is often coupled with a popular story of the ninth-century Sufi masters Rabia and Hasan of Basra. The much-loved Rabia and the well-known teacher Hasan were sitting under a tree discussing spiritual matters on the shore of a lake just outside a popular bazaar. Hasan was enamored of Rabia's beauty, so when it came time for prayers, Hasan unfurled his prayer rug and placed it on the water. Standing miraculously on the floating rug, Hasan casually invited Rabia to join him, hoping to impress her. Instead, Rabia spread out her prayer rug, perched on it, levitated above Hasan, and invited him to join her. She teased Hasan, "Isn't this what you want, for the people in the bazaar to see us and be stunned by our magical feat?" Rabia continued, "Hasan, what you did, a fish can do. What I did, a moth can do. You forget that what we are called to do is more difficult and more important: the work of transforming our beings."

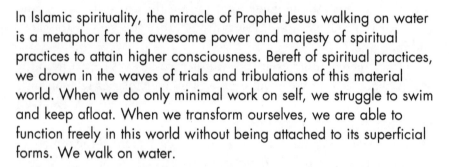

REFLECTIONS

In Islamic spirituality, the miracle of Prophet Jesus walking on water is a metaphor for the awesome power and majesty of spiritual practices to attain higher consciousness. Bereft of spiritual practices, we drown in the waves of trials and tribulations of this material world. When we do only minimal work on self, we struggle to swim and keep afloat. When we transform ourselves, we are able to function freely in this world without being attached to its superficial forms. We walk on water.

If you know the value of every article of merchandise but don't know the value of your own soul, it's all foolishness. (Rumi)

O Muslim, you do all kinds of rituals to protect yourself from the devil. But what if the devil is in your heart? O seeker of knowledge, you study all kinds of books. When will you study the most important book—the book that is you? (Traditional Sufi song)

You are veiled by your own self.[3] (Bistami)

PRACTICE

How would you articulate your mission in life?

Choose one personal practice you can do for fifteen minutes each day that will help you get in touch with something higher than your personality. It might be a short, mindful walk in the woods where you notice the natural world at play, a prayer practice, meditation, singing hymns, or chanting.

Some Shifts
in Awareness

The Storms in Our Lives

The Mulla was at the helm of a ferryboat loaded with scholars, lawyers, and businesspeople. It was a long journey and to pass the time they amused themselves watching the Mulla getting animated as he talked about God, the invisible realms, and the need to transform the ego and polish the heart. These were learned people with little faith in spiritual work and invisible worlds, and they chuckled merrily at the Mulla's expense. But midway in their journey, a storm arose and the ferry began to toss on the sea like a leaf in the air. Certain of their coming death, the people of reason got on their knees and implored God to save their lives. "I'll give You anything You ask," they promised. "I'll give up my riches, do pro bono work for the poor, reform my shady business practices"—the kind of bargaining we all do when we are desperate for divine help. The Mulla, calm and poised, walked between them and advised, "Friends! Now! Now! Be steady! Don't be so reckless with your goods." To the lawyers he said, "Come on, do your job well, drive a harder bargain!" To the businesspeople he noted, "Hey! What about the bottom line?" To the scholars he stated, "Really, you must do more research before making reckless promises." To all of them he teased, "Avoid entanglements with the invisible realms, as you have in your life so far." Suddenly, peering into the distance, the Mulla shouted, "Ahoy! Ahoy! I see land." The story ends with the passengers rising from their knees, celebrating, and entirely forgetting their desperate promises.

How like those passengers we are! We sail through life stuck in robotic patterns and showing little interest in the mysteries and purpose of our lives until the inevitable storms of life force us to get serious about that most basic of questions: What's it all about? But after the initial stirring of an inner awakening, many of us return to our slumber and our habitual patterns. The Qur'an laments: "Then comes a stormy wind and the waves come to them from all sides ... they sincerely cry unto Allah ... saying 'If thou dost deliver us from this, we shall truly show our gratitude!' But when He delivers them, behold! They transgress insolently through the Earth ..." (10:22–23).

Sufi teachers urge us to be more like the thoughtful minority of passengers on the Mulla's ferry, who were struck by his calm demeanor and asked if he hadn't realized that, in the violent storm, all that stood between them and death was a simple plank of wood. "Ah," the Mulla replied. "On land, in the course of daily life, there is even less between us and death, if only we knew."

We would do well to heed the Mulla's wisdom. One day, inevitably, our personal storms will not abate before causing destruction: the death of a family member, a cancer diagnosis, divorce, financial ruin—the possibilities are endless. Something will break our hearts and cause us to ask deeper questions. At that point we will become spiritual seekers, each in our own way. With the veils—or the simple wooden planks—of health and wealth ripped away, we will begin to hear deep inside the mysterious calling of our soul to fulfill the purpose for which we were created.

May we all become what Rumi called "early waking grievers." In Book 4 of the Masnavi, he quotes his favorite Andalusian poet, Adi Riga:

> I was sleeping and being comforted by a cool breeze, when suddenly a gray dove from the thicket sang and sobbed with longing, and reminded me of my own passion. I had been far away from my own soul so long, but that dove's crying woke me and made me cry! "Praise to all early waking grievers."

 REFLECTIONS

You shall certainly be tried in your possessions and in yourselves. (Qur'an 3:186)

Something missing in my heart tonight
Has made my eyes so soft,
My voice so tender
My need for God absolutely clear. (Hafiz)

Truly in the remembrance of God do hearts find peace. (Qur'an 13:28)

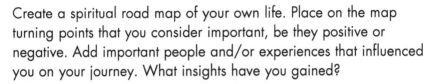

PRACTICE

Create a spiritual road map of your own life. Place on the map turning points that you consider important, be they positive or negative. Add important people and/or experiences that influenced you on your journey. What insights have you gained?

What changes have you made throughout your life journey as a result of your higher awareness? What else needs to be done?

Asking Deeper Questions

From earliest childhood we humans begin asking questions that have no easy answers. Who am I? Where did I come from? Why am I here? Why do people die? Where do people go when they die? Who is this "God" that people talk about? As we grow older, our questions might become more sophisticated and intense, but they are basically the same questions we asked when we daydreamed as five-year-old children lying at the base of a favorite tree and gazing up at the sky through a canopy of summer leaves. Now, as adults raking the leaves of autumn, we are still immersed in those childhood mysteries.

Poets and sages attempt to capture in words our sense of bafflement. "What was the mystery that made me open up like a little bud in the forest at midnight?" asks the twentieth-century Bengali poet Tagore.[1] "The lover visible, the Beloved invisible," Rumi cries. "Whose crazy idea was this?" Alas, none of our divine revelations arrive with footnotes or explanations. "Of knowledge We have given you but a little," says the Qur'an (17:85). That cryptic verse helps us to understand that we are not expected to know all the answers.

The Mulla knew very well our sense of bewilderment. One evening he spent many hours in the tavern drinking and talking with friends. In the early hours of the morning, in a state of intoxication, he wandered through the streets aimlessly. A policeman accosted him and asked, "Who are you? What are you doing at this unusual hour? Where did you come from? Where are you going?" "Sir," stammered the Mulla, "If I knew the answer to all those questions, I would be home already!" In Islamic spirituality, tavern and wine are symbols of gathering places where seekers acquire spiritual knowledge.

It is futile to search for definitive answers to life's deeper questions. What is fruitful is to simply be present with the Mystery of the questions as you go about your daily work. Perfume your heart with awe and wonder, say the mystics, and the rapture of the Mystery will awaken something deeper in you.

Can we mere mortals expect to obtain genuine insight into the mysteries of life? Consider the origins of the awe-inspiring wisdom in the Hindu scriptures. Hinduism teaches that there are four stages in the life of a human: student, householder, forest dweller, and wandering ascetic. In the forest-dwelling phase, husband and wife, after fulfilling their parental and otherworldly duties, retire literally or metaphorically into a forest to ponder the meaning and purpose of their lives. What was it all about? What was the purpose of all of the dramas and melodramas, joys and sorrows in their lives? Flashes of intuitive perception and glimpses of secrets beyond the veil were revealed to ordinary men and women who had reached that forest-dwelling phase of their lives. The collective wisdom of these "forest dwellers" forms an important part of Hindu scripture. For us, too, whether we go to the forest, the mountains, the ocean, or a quiet place in our own hearts, the insights are there if we would only be still and listen.

REFLECTIONS

With Him are the keys of the Unseen, the treasures that none knoweth but He. (Qur'an 6:59)

Sell your cleverness and buy bewilderment. Cleverness might be opinion, and bewilderment, naked vision. (Rumi)

The answer is inside the question. (Rumi)

PRACTICE

What are some of the awe-inspiring questions that arise in your heart?

If you have reflected on your questions, what kind of insights have you gained, and have they changed your patterns of thinking and behaving?

Write a poem or create a work of art or music that expresses your awe of the mystery of the Unseen.

Spirituality Is an Experience

One of the most frequently asked questions during presentations by the Interfaith Amigos (Rabbi Ted Falcon, Pastor Don Mackenzie, and I) is, "What is spirituality?" Pastor Don always answers with a quip: "That which pertains to spiritual matters." After the chuckles subside, he goes on to explain that the domain of spirituality is so vast that it defies a simple definition. There are, however, some common themes associated with spirituality: searching for self-knowledge and authentic meaning, exploring interconnectedness in the web of life, being of authentic service to God's creation, and opening ourselves to a higher power. One of my Sufi teachers defined spirituality as any practice or event that contributes to our transformative process. He often repeated the story of a famous teacher who actually paid an obnoxious member of a retreat he was leading to return after others, tired of his offensive behavior, had forced him to leave. The retreat master felt that the man's trying presence provided a good opportunity for the spiritual growth of the other retreat members. As the Qur'an says, "We have created some of you to be a trial for others" (25:20).

No matter how we define it, spirituality is experiential, not academic. It is rooted in the heart and must be felt and tasted deep inside. It is a Sufi maxim that "Those who taste, know." Numerous stories illustrate this basic truth. In one, the Mulla had a neighbor who repeatedly expressed interest in the study of spirituality and promised to make time to talk with him about these important matters, but the Mulla could see that the man thought spiritual knowledge could be transmitted simply by word of mouth. How could he show the neighbor how untrue that was? The opportunity came when the man shouted from his roof, "Mulla, could you please help me blow on the fire? The charcoal is dimming." "Of course!" the Mulla replied "My breath is always at your disposal. Come on over and take as much of my breath as you can carry back with you!"

A story related by the fifteenth-century Sufi teacher Jami also emphasizes the importance of personal experience in spiritual work. A well-known physician apprenticed her son to a Sufi master, but the master assigned the boy to clean the latrines. Hearing this, the mother begged the teacher to give her tender son a more worthy job and sent twelve Ethiopian slaves to clean the outhouses. The master sent the following reply: "You are a physician. If your son had an inflammation of the gallbladder, should I give the medicine to an Ethiopian slave instead of giving it to your son?"

And then there is the story about a man who was eager to receive the kind of adulation he had seen people lavish on Sufi masters. He sought out the Mulla and inquired about the length of the course to become a teacher. "Ten years," replied the Mulla. What if he studied twice as hard? "Twenty years," said the Mulla. What if he studied three times as hard? "Thirty years," came the reply. "How can that be?" asked the confused aspirant. "When one eye is fixated on fame and glory," said the Mulla, "there is only one eye left to find your way." Truly, the path of spirituality requires our full attention, along with patience, humility, sincerity, presence, and pure intentions.

Another Mulla story demonstrates that theories on spirituality are meaningless without personal experience. Strolling by the riverbank, the Mulla saw a man sitting with his neck bared to the sun. Eager to test a theory, he stretched out his arm and heartily slapped the man's neck, creating a whacking noise. As the man turned around to strike back, the Mulla said, "Before you get angry, tell me: The sound we heard, was it from the palm striking the neck or the neck receiving the blow?" "O silly theorist," replied the man, "the pain I feel leaves me no room for your speculations. You can afford them because you do not feel what I am feeling."

And finally, our friend Rumi cautions us not to get embroiled in unnecessary theological discussions. Doing that, he says, we are like a bird that ties and unties knots around its legs over and over again to show off its strange skill, forgetting that the point is to escape from the snare. "How sad it is that we have forgotten the joy and beauty of sailing the mountain air and smelling the sweetness of the high meadows!"

REFLECTIONS

External learning moves like a Moon and fades when the Sun of experience rises.[2] (Hakim Sanai)

Once we experience the Divine, our propensity to theorize is reduced remarkably.

Not all ecstasies are the same. Jesus was drunk on love for God; his donkey was drunk on barley. (Rumi)

PRACTICE

What experiences in your life have brought you closer to Presence, Mystery, Spirit, or God?

What are some ways you can sustain and deepen your connection to Mystery?

In Islamic spirituality, the heart is the main focus of spirituality. Try the simple technique of touching your heart as often as possible in your daily life, especially when expressing gratitude. Every morning, touch your heart and express gratitude to your Creator. Or touch your heart and simply be silent.

We Foolish Humans

It seems that we are always trying to understand other people, but how well do we know ourselves? Rumi warns that if we don't do the inner work, one of our main regrets on our deathbed may be that we are about to die without having tasted the water of our own essence. Knowing ourselves from the outside in is not enough. Consider the plight of the Mulla, who went with a friend on Hajj to Mecca. People from every corner of the world go on Hajj each year, all of them clothed in plain white robes, so the Mulla tied a conspicuous eggplant around his waist so that his friend would recognize him if they got separated. One evening after the Mulla fell asleep, a trickster untied the eggplant and fastened it around his own waist. When the Mulla awoke in the morning, he was confused. He saw the man with the eggplant and said, "I know who you are, but then, who am I?"

Each of us has to answer that question for ourselves, and it can take a lifetime to sift through the bewildering paradoxes of our human and divine natures. The Qur'an says we are molded from the basest of materials—clay—and yet infused with the divine breath of God (15:29). We have the weaknesses of human personality but also the infinite potential of divine identity. We can be hasty, foolish, and unjust, says the Qur'an, yet we were also chosen for the honor and responsibility of being God's vice-regents on earth. Endowed with free will, we can follow our lower instincts into debasement or ascend with our higher instincts into exaltation. Is it any wonder that we are confused about who we really are?

Who we really are, according to teachers from many traditions, is deceptively simple: We are all spiritual beings having a physical experience. We are rubies in the midst of granite, says Rumi. We are imbued with resplendent majesty but we insist on remaining shriveled and withered in our prison of dust. Why not become fresh from the gentleness of the heart's spring?, Rumi asks. Why not laugh like a rose? Why not spread perfume?

The truth is, we are fools. We don't realize our divine worth—
and we don't realize how foolish that is. We are too caught up in
the externals of life and the complications of our personalities. We
could learn from the Mulla, who agreed to teach a famous scholar
some techniques that would reveal insights beyond what books and
scriptures could offer. There was only one condition: For the first
week, the scholar's assignment was to kneel in the marketplace every
morning and evening, kiss the ground, grab his ears, and make a
particular sound. The scholar objected, but the Mulla reassured him
that this mysterious ritual would produce remarkable insights. A week
later the scholar returned to report his progress, and he was furious.
Everyone in the market had roared with laughter and derision. "I felt
like a fool!" he declared, "a total, complete fool!" "That's marvelous!"
exclaimed the Mulla. "For just one week's work, this is a profound
insight, wouldn't you say?"

You will be relieved to know that spiritual teachers are not
suggesting that we go to the market and make a fool of ourselves. But
they do suggest that we begin to surrender attachment to our daily
personality and begin to know ourselves as precious humans created
"in the best of molds" (Qur'an 95:4) and infused with the breath of
our Creator (Qur'an 32:9).

 # REFLECTION

We have indeed created man in the best of molds (Qur'an 95:4)
and He ... breathed into him something of His Spirit. (Qur'an 32:9)

 # PRACTICE

Do you believe that within you resides a divine essence and that
you can connect with it? Is there someone in your life who can
listen and support you when you talk about these topics and
experiences?

Have you ever had an experience, no matter how brief, where you
felt a joyous inner expansiveness and/or a connection with the web
of life? How did that affect your spiritual journey?

Three Stages of Knowing Oneself

"Know thyself," said the Prophet Muhammad, "and thou shalt know thy Lord." But this is not the simple self-knowledge exhibited by the Mulla when he went to a foreign bank to make a transaction. Asked by a bank officer to identify himself, the Mulla reached into his pocket, took out a small mirror, and studied it for several seconds. Then he announced with confidence, "Yes, that's me all right, I am happy to confirm it." No, what the Prophet and the Holy Qur'an urge upon us is the much more difficult task of getting to know our true selves, the divine self at the core of our being.

The pursuit of such self-knowledge is a central task in Sufi spirituality. It requires that we shine the compassionate light of awareness on ourselves as we go about our daily lives, trying consistently to become mindful of our bewildering inner paradoxes. The work is difficult, but if you abide with it gently and persistently, all the false selves will fall away and you will come face-to-face with the divine ruby within. That is your authentic self, and the more brightly the ruby shines, the more fully you are able to serve God's creation. You truly become God's vice-regent on earth.

The Qur'an suggests that our work is to transmute the ego by aligning it with our soul or higher self. This holy work proceeds in three main stages. First, we discover that our ego tends to be a commanding master and can incline us toward wrongdoing. Through abiding vigilance, we can transform the ego to become our personal assistant. This first stage can be as rewarding as it is to clear away the clutter in your office, basement, or garage: it's done in rather broad strokes and you really get a good sense of progress.

The second stage is more challenging, because it requires us to keep up the good habits and not let the useless ones pile up again. In this stage we become aware of the ego's cunning nature. We realize that we have choices, and through exploration and experience we learn discernment about our choices. We generally spend a good deal of time in this middle stage while ego and soul compete for our attention.

This is the stage the Mulla was in when he acquired such a reputation for his insightful sermons and devotional practices that the governor of the province began to attend his religious programs. After some time, the governor told the Mulla that he had benefited immensely from the programs and asked if there was anything he could do to return the favor. The Mulla thought for a minute, and then politely asked the governor not to attend the services for a while. Surprised, the governor asked if he had offended the Mulla in some way. "Not at all," said the Mulla. "The fault is mine. Before you started coming to services, I was praying and chanting only to please Allah. But now I'm more interested in pleasing you, because you might give me some earthly reward. So please, your honor, give me time to purify my motives, and then I will invite you to worship with us again."

In the last stage, we strive for spiritual maturity as we work to bring our semitamed ego in line with our higher self so that the ego is an instrument of the soul. Throughout this sacred process, the point has been not to destroy or discard the ego, but to transmute it by expanding it into a higher will. As our self-knowledge steadily increases, we begin to realize that in subtle ways the ego wants us to fulfill our life's purpose by moving beyond it and opening into a greater fullness. The ego is like an autumn garden in which next spring's growth is concealed. If we continuously shine the light of awareness, spring will arrive and the garden will burst into bloom.

The wise tell us that once we commit ourselves to this work, we receive help from the invisible realms. The All-Compassionate One wants us to attain joy and fulfillment. We are touched by Grace. "Take one step toward Him and He takes seven steps toward you," the Prophet said. "Walk to Him and He comes running."

❧ REFLECTIONS ❧

The three stages of the ego named in the Qur'an are as follows:

nafs al-ammarah, or headstrong ego, also called commanding master (12:53) *nafs al-lawwama,* or self-reproaching ego (75:2)

nafs al-mutma'inna, or ego at peace (89:27)

Those who are controlled by their lower self must serve it; those who control the lower ego serve others. (Hazrat Ali)

One does not become enlightened by imagining figures of light, but by making the darkness conscious.[3] (Carl Jung)

PRACTICE

How well do you know yourself? What steps do you take to develop a relationship with yourself?

Keep a notebook with you at all times. When you notice yourself displaying certain traits, whether ego or divine, make a note of it. For example, when you feel a twinge of jealousy, mark it down. And if you find yourself acting with compassion, mark that down also. At the end of the day, look at what you noted. Allow yourself to feel gratitude for your growing awareness of your personal traits, both ego and divine. Slowly but surely, the light of consciousness will diminish your shadow and illuminate your beautiful qualities.

Foibles and
Vulnerabilities

Seeking Approval from Others

The human yearning for love and approval is innate and deep. Whenever we meet someone, says the poet Hafiz, a voice inside us cries out, "Love me! O, please love me!" All this happens silently, of course. Otherwise, says Hafiz, someone would call the authorities to lock us up!

Our eagerness to receive approval from others, and the cartwheels we turn to obtain it, can be frustrating and exhausting. Consider the Mulla's attempts to please his critics as he ambled with his grandson and his donkey through the marketplace. "Hey, what's the matter with you?" shouted someone in the crowd. "Two journeyers and a healthy beast of burden, but you insist on tiring yourselves out by walking?" So the Mulla mounted the donkey, but down the road he overheard people saying, "It's no wonder our younger generation is disgruntled and disrespectful. The man on the donkey is old enough to be wise in years, but he lets the boy, tender in years, suffer under the searing sun." The Mulla quickly dismounted and perched his grandson on the beast of burden. Further along the path, more whispers: "Just imagine! A perfectly robust boy is enthroned on the donkey while the grandfather shuffles under the scorching heat. How we spoil our young ones and then wonder why they grow up so brash and demanding." Hearing this, both the Mulla and grandson got on the donkey, but then another conversation reached their ears. "How merciless! Silently, the poor donkey suffers under the burden of the young and old. Surely, the Heavens will punish us all for the way we abuse Allah's dumb creatures." To silence the critics, both grandfather and grandson disembarked, lifted up the donkey, balanced him on their shoulders, and started walking. This, of course, only elicited more scorn and advice.

What do we learn from this amusing story? First, there is the truism that has been taught for centuries in many traditions: "Whosoever approval you seek, you are their prisoner." This is a law of the created world; it has nothing to do with good or bad, right or wrong. The insight is about self-awareness. In your life, whose approval are you seeking, whether consciously or unconsciously? The answer may provide many clues about the quality of your life.

In my youth, my teachers had me meditate for days and weeks on this simple but profound insight. Whenever I felt I had plumbed its depths, my teachers ascertained that my comprehension was glib and superficial. Only when they felt that my heart had a glimpse of the truth of this insight did they disclose a second one: "Choose your jailors with care and deliberation." Because, as stated at the beginning of this chapter, it is human nature to seek love and approval, we must choose individuals and institutions that embody values that resonate in our hearts: love, compassion, truth, graciousness, patience, and courage. "Keep company with those who remind you of God," says the tenth-century Sufi teacher Ibn Khafif, "and seek approval of those who counsel not with the tongue of words but the tongue of deeds."[1]

If you must have a jailor, say the Sufis, let God be your jailor. Speak and act in ways that are pleasing to your Sustainer. Sing for God, who embodies attributes of divine beauty. Sing as if you were the unnamed teacher of the famous musician Tansen, who awed the court of the sixteenth-century Mughal emperor Akbar.

When Tansen sang, legends say, birds stopped chirping and tree branches bowed in sweet respect. Emperor Akbar was so enthralled with Tansen's singing that he begged the musician to introduce him to his teacher. On the way to the cave where the teacher lived, the emperor heard the master sing. Such was the beauty of the sound that the emperor swooned into unconsciousness. When he was revived, he turned to Tansen and exclaimed, "Tansen! Tansen! Your voice is magical. But what I experienced today is the music of the spheres. It is divine! Tansen, why can't you sing like your teacher? What gives his voice this unutterable beauty?" Tansen replied, "My emperor, the reason is simple. I sing for you. My master sings for that Supreme Majesty, the Emperor of emperors. That is what makes his voice so unique."

I realized the deep meaning of this story when I met an elderly Christian minister who had spent over forty years in Africa trying, at the behest of his religious superiors, to counter Islamic preachers who were converting the locals to Islam. Lamenting what he called "those wasted years," he talked about how he had obeyed his superiors in strategizing, scheming, and arguing to serve the kingdom of Caesar—the realm of political and ecclesiastical power—and not the kingdom of God. How he wished that he might get back those years and spend them becoming more like Jesus and less like Caesar!

REFLECTION

One person belongs to many masters and suffers from their many quarrels, says the Qur'an (39:29), while another belongs to a single master who allows him to focus on the pursuit of goodness. Which one is happier?, asks the Holy Book. The answer is clear in a later Sura: Seeking only the Face of thy Lord Most High, that one will know peace of mind. (Qur'an 92:20–21)

PRACTICE

Who are the people and institutions whose approval you seek? Write down their names. In each case, examine whether this person or institution exemplifies the values and ethics you believe in.

If you need to change your "jailor," craft a simple affirmation or ritual that grounds and connects you in a compassionate and sacred way to your new commitment.

Clinging to an Image

In our relationships with others, we play a variety of roles. We might be a parent, partner, professional, and party clown all rolled into one. If our personality is integrated, our roles flow smoothly without too much strain. But if the aspects of our personality are not cohesive and assimilated, we often force ourselves to wear masks in our dealings with others, and this can be exhausting. First we have to calculate what kind of face will have the desired effect, and then we have to wear it, even if it doesn't reflect who we really are deep inside. We become prisoners of our images, unable to express the simple truth of who we are.

A few years ago, I was privileged to experience the gentle humor of the Dalai Lama and Archbishop Desmond Tutu at an interfaith breakfast in Seattle. Like innocent children, the two luminaries joked and bantered with each other and broke into prolonged peals of laughter. Suddenly, Archbishop Tutu became serious and said to the Dalai Lama, "Your holiness, this laughter must stop! After all, our guests think we are holy people. We have an image to uphold." At that, we all roared with laughter.

Truly holy people do not need to act as if they are holy. Their sacred essence flows from the inside out in every situation and relationship. Because of the spiritual work they have done, they have moved from habitual masks to their real face. As Rumi says, "Your real face is so beautiful if only you knew." At our core, there is perfection. When we are in touch with that perfection, we manifest kindness naturally, without having to think about it.

But what happens if we continuously uphold a self-image that is rooted not in our essence but in our vain desire for fame or good public opinion? We become constrained to do things that are not in our highest interest. That is what happened to Aga Akil, who was known as a holy man in the Mulla's village. One day the Mulla saw him rushing home in a downpour and shouted at him, "How can you, a holy man, be fleeing from God's bounty? Does not the Qur'an say that the waters pouring from the Heavens are a sign of mercy and a sacred gift from God?" Anxious to maintain his reputation, Aga Akil raised both hands to praise Allah and slowed down his pace. The next day he caught a chill. That day it poured again and through his window, he noticed the Mulla rushing home. "Why are you running away from God's blessings?" shouted the holy man. "Have you no respect for divine gifts?" The Mulla replied, "It is precisely for that reason that I am hastening home. I do not want to defile the sacred waters with my feet!"

REFLECTION

It's too bad that you want to be someone else. You don't see your own face, your own beauty. Yet, no face is more beautiful than yours. (Rumi)

PRACTICE

In which areas of your life do you feel a need to hold on to an image? Whose approval are you seeking? Why is it important to you? Does this image reflect your true identity, or an identity you or someone else has conjured up?

If the image you wish to uphold bears a quality you truly want to evolve into, create an affirmation about it and repeat it to yourself again and again as often as possible. If you yearn to project an image of yourself as a compassionate human being, you might tell yourself repeatedly, "My true self is filled with the divine light of compassion. I am compassionate within and without." Seize every opportunity to behave with compassion. A sincere application of this simple practice will inspire and lead you to additional spiritual practices, and connect you to that quality in a real way. Your image will be a reflection of who you really are.

Slavish Dependence on Authorities and Experts

When we are feeling insecure and have little faith in ourselves, we often place too much faith in external authorities in every area of our lives. Dazzled by titles and academic degrees, we defer to experts and pundits in forming our opinions and beliefs. The Mulla learned the danger of such blind faith as he lay gravely ill, surrounded by family, friends, and his wailing wife. The doctor arrived and a hush came over the room as he examined the Mulla. After quite some time the doctor turned to the Mulla's wife and declared, "O honorable wife of the Mulla, only Allah is immortal. It is with deep sorrow that I have to inform you that your husband has passed away. He is dead. His soul has flown to the bosom of God." As the doctor continued his eloquent remarks, the Mulla feebly protested, "No, wait! I'm alive! I'm alive!" "Quiet!" retorted his wife, "The doctor is speaking. Don't argue with the doctor!"

The story continues with the Mulla being carried in an open coffin to his gravesite, surrounded by a large funeral procession. The Mulla, who was still alive, suddenly sat up and a debate ensued among the members of the community as to whether he was alive or dead. An ad hoc committee was created on the spot to discuss this strange happening. An elder passed around the certificate of the doctor, declaring him dead. This authoritative piece of paper was sufficient to settle the issue. The learned committee declared that it was their expert belief that the Mulla was indeed dead. The Mulla was duly informed, whereupon he dutifully lay down and the procession continued.

On the way to the gravesite, someone brought up an important theological question. In Islam, are mourners supposed to walk on the right or left side of the coffin? Is it permissible to walk in front or back of the coffin? Again the procession stopped and a fatwa was called for. (A fatwa is a scholarly opinion issued by an expert in Islamic religious law on a specific issue. In theory, the institution of Islam has no priesthood, religious hierarchy, or religious ordination. The definition of a religious expert in Islam is vague. Thankfully, fatwas are nonbinding and those who know this often go "fatwa shopping" to find support for a preferred point of view.) In the Mulla's processional group, many claimed to be experts and shouted a variety of opinions until the Mulla could stand it no longer. Sitting up again, he declared, "I hereby issue a fatwa that it is permitted in Islam for a living person to walk right, left, front, or back of the coffin as long as that person is not inside the coffin!"

Like the characters in the Mulla stories, some of us are practically addicted to the words of religious experts and surrender our common sense even when reality clashes with belief. Many teaching stories illustrate the absurdity of this dependence. In one such story, a group of religious men went to the Mulla to ask for a ruling. They planned to strip to their shorts and wade in the sea. Should they orient their faces to the right or left side? Replied the Mulla, "Turn your faces to the spot where your clothes are!"

REFLECTIONS

Even if the religious judge advises you about earthly matters, first consult your heart. (*Hadith*)

Are you aware of the authorities and experts in your life who shape your beliefs and opinions?

PRACTICE

In a meditative state, place two conflicting opinions or beliefs one at a time inside your heart. Become aware of feelings that come up. Lean toward the one that brings peace and harmony to your being.

In what other ways can you "consult your heart"?

Swayed by Outer Forms

The Qur'an sternly cautions us not to be misled by externals of title and power. In a chapter titled "He frowned," the Holy Book describes an incident when the Prophet Muhammad was explaining the tenets of Islam to a powerful but arrogant Arab chieftain. This was a crucial conversation because the embryonic Muslim community needed allies to survive, so the Prophet was annoyed when a poor, blind, elderly man interrupted to ask a question about the Qur'an. The Prophet frowned, the Qur'an says, and soon afterward he received a revelation:

> *And the one who regards himself as self-sufficient*
> *To him you pay attention....*
> *But as for the one who came eagerly to you*
> *And with an inner awe*
> *Him you disregarded. (80:5–10)*

The Prophet, an ardent advocate for the poor and marginalized, was mortified and deeply repentant. From that day forward, he always acknowledged the old man with respect and honor, and the man was so touched that he joined the Muslim community. History records that he went on to become the governor of Medina.

If the Prophet needed a divine reminder not to be swayed by the trappings of rank and power, so much more do we mortals need to pay attention to this human flaw. The Mulla knew this lesson very well, and had a good time teaching it to the officials at the king's annual banquet. He arrived dressed as a peasant, and the chief of protocol seated him in an inconspicuous place close to the end of the line. Eager to be served more quickly, he went home and returned dressed in a magnificent sable cloak and turban. Sure enough, the chief of protocol ordered drums to be rolled and trumpets to be sounded for this high-ranking guest, and the king's chamberlain seated him close to the king. When the food arrived, the Mulla began to rub handfuls of food into his cloak and turban. "Your Excellency," remarked the king, "I am always eager to learn local customs. Pray, tell me more about your eating rituals, which are new to me." The Mulla replied, "It is a custom in our province to give everything its due share. Since it was my cloak and turban that got me such a choice place at the table, I'm making sure that they get their just deserts."

Our reverence for symbolic cloaks and turbans can be misplaced, as the Mulla demonstrated in yet another story about the disconnect between inner knowledge and external trappings. An illiterate villager received an official letter and asked the Mulla to read it to him, but the Mulla said he had learned to write but not to read. "Then how dare you wear that turban?" the villager demanded, since he assumed that the turban signaled that he was a person of learning. The Mulla immediately took off his turban and put it on the villager's head, saying, "Here, go ahead and read the letter now!"

REFLECTIONS

Do not, through giving, seek thyself to gain, but unto your Sustainer turn in patience. (Qur'an: 74:6–7)

There is form and there is essence. Do not confuse one with the other. (Traditional saying)

How do you treat people in your life who offer you no material benefit or advantage?

To what ends do you go to impress others? Whom do you wish to impress, and why?

PRACTICE

Take honest stock of the kinds of people you choose to befriend. Examine the underlying reasons for your choices, and if they are merely self-serving, take steps to adopt more worthy criteria for your relationships.

Appetite for Praise and Titles

The human ego has an endless appetite for praise and lofty titles. The Prophet Muhammad recognized the spiritual dangers of this flaw and repeatedly told his followers that he was simply a servant and messenger of God. "You are our master," the members of a tribal delegation once said to him, and he replied, "God is your master." Continuing their obeisance, they said, "You are the most excellent of the highest degree." But he replied, "Do not exceed reasonable bounds in praise."[2]

Sadly, as Islam spread across the world and Muslim rulers established a global empire, the Prophet's warnings began to fall on deaf ears. Rulers, princes, and even local feudal lords began a tradition of employing poets and singers to compose and sing epic verses of praise and honor to them. Titles such as "God Gifted," "God Accepted," and "God Exalted" became commonplace. But the Mulla came up with a unique solution when a local prince employed him to compose a title. It had to be succinct, invoke the name of God, and reflect the outstanding qualities of the prince. Most of all, it had to be unique. After much thought and meditation, the Mulla announced an appropriate title: "God Forbid"!

When we do good work with our God-given gifts, what is our true motivation? Is it to glorify our Creator, or is it to astound the world with our brilliance? Look deeply into your heart, says the twelfth-century mystic Al-Ghazzali, for on Judgment Day the truth will be laid bare and all our hypocrisies will be exposed. On that day, God will question the learned about what they did with the gift of knowledge conferred on them. They will reply, "We spent it in your way." But the Lord will say, "You spent it to earn applause and be known as the learned." When the wealthy are asked what they did with the riches God gave them, they will say, "We spent them in your way." But God will say, "You spent them so that people would call you benevolent and charitable." Then God will ask those who gave their lives in holy wars, "How did you spend the life I gave you?" They will reply, "We sacrificed ourselves for your sake." But God will reply, "You gave away your lives so that people would call you brave and honor you as martyrs."[3]

Even the legendary ninth-century caliph Harun al-Rashid, known for his wisdom, needed reminders not to be waylaid by praise and pomposity. Donning expensive robes and symbols of power, he rode with fanfare in the streets during a festival, savoring his subjects' praise and ovations. But then his path was barred by the "wise fool" Bahlul, his favorite court jester. Knowing that he had free rein to speak openly to the caliph, Bahlul dared to say that the royal festival is not about dressing up ostentatiously and receiving personal praise. The festival is celebrated by being conscious of God and serving God's creation. To celebrate the festival is to be Sultan of the heart, not Sultan of the realm. "Sultans of the realm pass into oblivion," said Bahlul, "but the Sultan of the heart is never forgotten." It is reported that these words brought Harun al-Rashid to tears.[4]

Ultimately, our inner work will bring us to a place where we can experience both adulation and censure without feeling overly giddy or painfully squeezed. As we strive to subdue and transform our egos, let us model ourselves after the wise man in the following story told in the villages of South Asia. This man lived such a life of service that the people of the village praised him to his face: "You are an angel! You are a true friend of God! How blessed we are that you eat and sleep among us." To all their praise, the man softly said, "Is that right?" But then a scandal brewed: The unwed daughter of the village chief became pregnant and claimed that the holy man was the father of her baby. Enraged, the villagers gathered around his hut hurling threats and insults: "You scum of the earth! You are a degenerate and a hypocrite!" Adults spat on him and children threw stones, but to all their scorn he simply replied, "Is that right?" After many years his accuser was afflicted with an incurable disease and made a deathbed confession: "May God forgive me, for I lied about the holy man. He is not the father of my child. It was someone else." Deeply repentant, the villagers assembled around his hut and showered him again with praise: "You are a celestial being. You are divine." And again the righteous man gently replied, "Is that right?"

What is the righteous response when someone praises us or confers an honor that we have not sought? Spiritual teachers advise us to be gracious and offer sincere thanks to the giver, but also give silent praise and gratitude to the Grand Giver and offer a prayer from your heart that your talents and good qualities may be used in service to God's creation. Beyond that, the Qur'an suggests that you whisper in your heart, *Estaghfirullah,* or "I beg repentance" to counter the ego's natural tendency to gloat or think it has earned adulation through its own merit. From God we receive our gifts, and to God belongs the glory.

REFLECTIONS

To God belong the most beautiful names. (Qur'an 59:24)

Those saved from the covetousness of their own souls, they are the ones who achieve prosperity. (Qur'an 59:9)

So do not claim purity for yourselves—He knows best who is conscious of Him. (Qur'an 53:32)

Titles, riches, and awards will have to be left behind in your palace at the moment of death. Friends and family can accompany you only up to the gravesite. Beyond that what carries you forward are authentic righteous deeds. (Traditional saying)

PRACTICE

Can you name a quality in yourself that has been praised by others? Take time to touch your heart and express gratitude for this divine quality flowing through you.

When you praise someone, make sure it comes from a place of sincerity in you. Silently, offer a prayer for the person you are praising. May Divinity make that beautiful attribute thrive in the person's being.

Know and Laugh at Your Eccentricities

The faithful are mirrors to each other, said the Prophet Muhammad: What we like or dislike in others is a reflection of what we appreciate and disapprove of in ourselves. Similarly, the eccentricities that amuse us in others often have their counterpart in our own behaviors. But our peculiarities are no laughing matter! Ours are meaningful, and we are attached to them. We enjoy our complaints and the sympathy they elicit. Why let go of them, when they are so rewarding? We complain of our maladies, but delay or refuse treatment for them.

We are like the Mulla, who complained to his family and friends that his sleep was disrupted because he kept dreaming every night that he was having wrestling matches with donkeys. Finally, they persuaded him to see a famous healer for treatment. The healer prepared a special herbal mixture, read some Qur'anic verses over the medicine, and said, "Take this tonight and rest assured that your donkey dreams will disappear forever." The Mulla expressed gratitude but asked, "Can I take this tomorrow night?" "Why not tonight?" inquired the healer. Replied the Mulla, "Because tonight I am scheduled to wrestle in the finals of the championship match!"

In another story, the Mulla took his donkey to the marketplace and put it up for sale. But every time a customer approached, the donkey kicked and bit the potential buyer. Finally, someone asked the Mulla how he expected to sell his donkey if the animal exhibited such difficult behavior. To his surprise, the Mulla replied, "Actually, I have no intention of selling my donkey. I just want people to know what I have to put up with all day long!"

Sometimes we manipulate universal human eccentricities to our advantage. To earn extra money, the Mulla took to begging in the town square. Soon he attracted a large crowd. People from faraway came to witness a strange phenomenon. No matter how often people offered a large and small coin, he always chose the smaller piece.

People shook their heads in disbelief and laughed heartily at his foolishness.

One day a kind man came to him and whispered, "Mulla, you should take the larger coin. This way you will have more money and you will not be a laughingstock of the town." The Mulla whispered back, "Actually, if I took the larger amount, people will stop offering me money. They continue to give me the money only to prove to themselves that I am more idiotic than they are!"

There is another eccentric trait we have to be mindful about. When we first receive urgently needed help, we are happy, relieved, and grateful. When the help continues, it is amazing how quickly we take it for granted and consider it our entitlement. Sometimes we, like the Mulla, take advantage of that kind of help whether it comes from individuals or institutions. The president of the Mulla's factory called a meeting and told all the employees that from next month the factory would be completely automated. There were gasps of disbelief and people shouted, "But how will we feed our families?" "Please don't be alarmed," the president said. "All of you have been loyal employees. You will no longer work here, but here is the fantastic news. Because of the increased profits, you will be paid as usual with annual increments! You will continue to enjoy the subsidized cafeteria and sports facilities. All you have to do is to come in on Fridays to collect your pay." There were sighs of relief, tears of joy, and much laughter. After a while, the Mulla raised his hand and asked, "That's great, but not every Friday, I hope?"

 # REFLECTIONS

The burden of self is lightened when I laugh at myself. (Tagore)

But the human being ... was indeed unjust and foolish.
(Qur'an 33:72)

 # PRACTICE

Think about the foibles of others that amuse you and ask yourself honestly if you also exhibit some of those same foibles. Allow yourself to laugh.

Make a list of other eccentricities you notice in yourself. Do it in a spirit of play. Are there any secondary benefits in holding on to them?

How do you consciously or unconsciously take advantage of the quirks of others?

Whose generosity and help do you take for granted? Do you feel that you have been sufficiently grateful? What changes in your attitude and behavior might be more optimal?

Excuse after Excuse

We all make excuses for our various lapses and laziness, but have you ever stopped to think that excuses are a form of lying? Just listen to the Mulla with his excuses when a neighbor asked to borrow his donkey. "I'm so sorry," said the Mulla, "but I just lent it to someone else. I wish you had come an hour earlier." Then suddenly the Mulla's donkey in the stable began to bray. The neighbor exclaimed, "But Mulla, I can hear your donkey!" Feigning outrage, the Mulla replied angrily, "Who will you believe—me or the donkey?" Closing the door, the Mulla muttered, "A friend who believes the word of a donkey above my own doesn't deserve to be lent anything!"

In fact, the Mulla is full of excuses, some of them positively absurd. Yearning to eat a ripe mango, he hoisted his ladder over the wall of a mango orchard. "What are you doing here?" demanded the gardener who arrived unexpectedly. "I am here to sell ladders and have brought a sample," replied the Mulla. "What nonsense, you know that this is no place to sell ladders!" said the gardener. The Mulla shot back, "It is you who doesn't understand. A ladder can be sold anywhere and at any time. These are the basic elements of successful salesmanship."

In another story the Mulla quietly trespassed onto a rich farm one stormy night and was busy stuffing his sack with fruits and vegetables when suddenly the owner appeared and demanded that the Mulla explain himself. "A high wind blew me here," the Mulla said. When the owner asked how it was that some of the vegetables were uprooted, the Mulla recounted with some flair how he had to grab onto them to prevent himself from being blown away. And when the owner demanded to know how the vegetables had gotten inside his sack, the Mulla calmly replied, "Indeed, that is the stuff of mystery. This is exactly the question I was pondering before you so rudely interrupted me."

Sometimes we impose on others to deliver our excuses and don't fully realize how absurd and transparent our lies are. The Mulla went to a castle to ask for donations for a worthwhile charity. The doorkeeper received his request, went inside for a while, and returned with the message that the owner of the castle was away on tour. "Oh really," replied the Mulla, "Then please deliver a message from me to your master. Even though he has not made any contribution, he can have this invaluable advice for free. Next time he leaves the castle, please tell him that he should not leave his face looking out the window. Somebody might steal it!"

And then there are the times we trip ourselves up by being too proud of our own cleverness. One evening during conversations with friends at the teahouse, the Mulla impulsively invited them to his house for dinner to continue the camaraderie. So they trooped to the Mulla's house and waited at the door while the Mulla went inside to inform his wife that she had a dozen guests to feed. She angrily told him there was barely enough food for the two of them, but the Mulla argued that his reputation was at stake and they had to do something. So they decided to wait, hoping the friends would get restless and go away. Instead, the friends knocked on the door. Opening the door, the wife told them the Mulla was not at home. "But how is that possible?" one of them asked. "We saw him go in through the door and we have been here all this time." The wife was silent but the Mulla, unable to contain himself, blurted out, "I could have gone out by the back door, you know!"

In the course of Sufi training, the Mulla stories about excuses are a prelude to serious reflection on the classical work of the thirteenth-century teacher Fariduddin Attar, titled "Conference of the Birds." This brilliant allegory illuminates, among other insights, the variety of excuses we invoke to avoid working to improve ourselves and to remove the obstacles from our path. All the birds of the world have assembled and are pouring out their dissatisfaction and disenchantment. They have realized that their mysterious thirst and inner ache is about a yearning to meet with their king and creator, the Simurgh. To their utter delight, the hoopoe bird, a confidant of Solomon and messenger of invisible realms, is familiar with the path to the Simurgh. The birds twitter and chirp with excitement. They are seized with an intense longing to travel to the abode of their Lord straightaway!

But then the hoopoe tells them about the perils of the journey. The Path traverses seven hazardous valleys named Quest, Love,

Understanding, Detachment, Unity, Bewilderment, and finally, Annihilation. In each valley a hundred difficulties will assail the seekers! In short, the path is long and the sea is deep. At every stage seekers must have the heart of a lion. One by one the birds, according to their circumstances and needs, begin to articulate their excuses. The nightingale is so in love with the rose that she cannot think of her own existence. "The love of the rose is enough for the nightingale," she says. The peacock displays his glittering plumage, struts with pride, and confesses that it is his destiny to live in the earthly Paradise; nothing else has any meaning for him. The sparrow pleads that she has neither down nor feathers. How can a weakling like her survive such an arduous flight? On and on the birds present their excuses not to undertake the journey to their soul's true Delight, and the hoopoe has a stinging rebuke for each one. A rose bloom lasts a single season and is no more; earthly pleasure is nothing compared with heavenly bliss; the difficulties they will encounter are no worse than what any other birds must endure.

And we? What are our excuses? Whatever we come up with, we should be aware that they truly hurt our souls. "Souls love the truth," say the Sufi sages, and when we construct an intricate scaffolding of mini-lies to support our misalignments, this puts an enormous strain on the soul. We can be just as creative as the Mulla when it comes to excuses for avoiding our spiritual work, but if we used the same ingenuity and persistence to "just do it," we probably would become enlightened in half the time!

 # REFLECTION

What excuses have you to offer, my heart, for so many shortcomings? (Rumi)

 # PRACTICE

Become aware of your excuses. Reflect on what you excuse yourself from, and how. Take note of how much time, energy and creativity you invest in making excuses for yourself.

Make a list of your habitual excuses. With mercy for self, and with persistence, give yourself permission to look at your excuses. Allow yourself to laugh! But make sure that you look at them in their fullness. You may see a common pattern in your excuses. The gentle light of awareness will, over time, expose the pattern, and dissolve it. This could significantly change the course of your life.

Truth of Convenience

The Mulla was cooking for a party and asked to borrow a large pot from the woman next door. She was reluctant to lend the pot, but felt obligated by the laws of hospitality and grudgingly let him borrow it. To her surprise, the Mulla returned the pot promptly, along with a smaller pot. The large pot must have been pregnant when he borrowed it, he explained, and it gave birth to the little one. "Oh, my," replied the delighted housewife, "I did have a faint suspicion about this." She thanked the Mulla profusely for taking care of the delivery. When the Mulla returned a few months later to borrow the large pot again, the housewife happily parted with it. But in the following days there was no sign of the Mulla and when the housewife went to collect her pot, the Mulla with much sadness explained that the pot had been pregnant again but, alas, this time it died in childbirth. "That's ridiculous!" replied the housewife. "How can a pot possibly become pregnant and then die in childbirth?" "Ah, but Madam," replied the Mulla, "you believed me the first time the pot was pregnant. So we did establish that pots are mortal, and surely, unexpected deaths are tragic but not uncommon."

In this classic story, both the Mulla and the housewife were seeking their own advantage by telling and accepting what Sufis call "truths of convenience"—manipulations of the truth for personal advantage. The untamed ego loves to play games with the truth. Think of the little lies and excuses we make up daily in the form of a slightly bent truth, exaggeration, avoidance, or denial. Then there are the bigger and outright lies we tell ourselves to justify our biases and advance our own interests. Every time we lie or engage in truths of convenience, we widen the gap between ourselves and our true essence.

In another story, the Mulla was serving as a village judge when his neighbor approached him for a legal opinion. "If your bull gored and hurt my cow, do I have any legal recourse?" "Of course not," replied the Mulla quickly. "An animal cannot be held responsible for its actions." The neighbor sighed in relief. "I'm glad to hear that. But actually, I got the story backwards. What I really meant to say was that *my* bull gored *your* cow." "That is a completely different set of circumstances!" exclaimed the Mulla. "In that case I must do more research and check legal precedents before making a pronouncement!"

Since it is easy to lapse into maneuvering the truth to serve our interests, how do we check this habit of the ego? The wise ask us to examine our intentions and sincerity before speaking and taking action on our truth.

An elderly Muslim once confided to me about how he distorted the truth to suit his personal convenience. In his thirties he decided to take a second wife. He justified his action on the basis of *sunnah,* or example of the Prophet, who had several wives. Not only was it his right, he said, it was his sacred mission to give multiple women marital protection and provision. The truth was that he lusted after a younger woman. Years later, the man's son married an older woman who was a divorcée, and the man was so outraged by the "shame" his son was bringing on the family by marrying such a woman that he disinherited him. The son, also citing *sunnah,* pointed out that the Prophet's beloved first wife, Khadija, was fifteen years his senior and a divorcée. This time the sacred conduct of the Prophet was of no interest to the father and he remained estranged from his son for some years. By grace of God, the man attended a conference on forgiveness and came to realize that his use of *sunnah* for his own marriage and his rejection of *sunnah* in the case of his son's marriage had really been examples of "truths of convenience." With this realization he was able to connect with his most authentic self and was lovingly reconciled with his son.

As harmful as it is to our own souls when we manipulate the truth, it can be even more damaging when religions and governments propagate "truths of convenience." Religious institutions and clerics have been known to unabashedly interpret scripture to support the vested interests of those in power.

Thus it is not surprising that today, in the era of the Arab Spring, when the populations of Arab countries are challenging their authoritarian governments, jurists are issuing new "truths of convenience" at the behest of the beleaguered leaders. Religious authorities in Saudi Arabia have issued rulings that the popular overthrow of an existing government is un-Islamic, while those in

Egypt have declared that the uprising in their country is in full conformity with the teachings of the Qur'an and *hadith*. The Mulla well knew the fallacy of these religious "truths": Asked if his religion was orthodox, he replied, "That depends on which bunch of heretics is in power."

Individually or collectively, it is difficult to discern when we begin to fabricate a "truth of convenience." We need to examine our deepest intentions with heart and soul. Are we speaking from our highest selves when we give an excuse or render an opinion that works to our advantage?

REFLECTIONS

Be ever steadfast in upholding equity, bearing witness to the truth for the sake of God, even though it be against your own selves or your parents and kinsfolk. Whether the person concerned be rich or poor, God's claim takes precedence over the claims of either of them. Do not, then, follow your own desires, lest you swerve from justice: for if you distort the truth, behold, God is indeed aware of all that you do. (Qur'an 4:135)

Seekers there are in plenty: but they are almost all seekers of personal advantage. I find so few seekers of truth.[5] (Hakim Jami)

Souls love the truth. (Traditional Sufi saying)

PRACTICE

What are some truths of convenience, little or big, that you engage in? What are some gentle steps you can take, little by little, to substitute unvarnished truth for these truths of convenience?

Attached to the Familiar

Employed as a court adviser, the Mulla encountered a royal falcon for the first time and thought what an odd-looking pigeon it was. Thinking to be of service, he trimmed the claws, wings, and beak of the falcon until, crowing with satisfaction, he declared, "Finally, you look like a decent pigeon. Obviously, your keeper was neglecting you."

How often we behave like the Mulla in our encounters with the unfamiliar! How attached we can be to our conditioned beliefs, attitudes, and preferences! The influences of family, tribe, religion, and media define many of our perceptions and reinforce our attachment to them. Our understanding and appreciation of the other is in direct proportion to what is familiar to us. Often we try to fix and fit the other into our "culture," "religion," and "way of life." We cut the person to fit the cloth. This cliché is a sharp and cutting metaphor, but it is indicative of the harm we cause when we are limited in our worldview.

Ours is a huge, magnificent world, brimming with beauty, variety, and diversity. What we perceive is a minuscule fraction of the fraction of what really exists. Rumi says that if a drop of the wine of vision could rinse our eyes, everywhere we looked, we would weep with wonder. Sadly, many of us are stuck in the confines of our tribal culture and beliefs and are astonishingly unaware of the splendor that lies beyond what we know. We are like the well frog in a classic story about two frogs with vastly differing perspectives on the size of the ocean.

An ocean frog was visiting his cousin, a well frog, and was trying to describe the vastness of the ocean. "Are you saying that the ocean is as large as half the size of this well?" asked the well frog in disbelief. "Oh, larger," said the ocean frog. "You don't mean to say that your ocean is as large as this well!" "Much larger." "That's impossible!" exclaimed the frog who had lived in the well most of his life. "That's just impossible!" When the skeptical well frog returned his cousin's visit and saw the size of the ocean, his head exploded, it is said, because he was not able to accept the vastness of this truth!

One of the best ways to expand our awareness is to travel and experience a variety of unfamiliar cultures: savor different foods, observe different customs, and learn the different worldviews of our cousins in the human family. The Qur'an refers to this essential life practice several times. "God has spread out the earth as a carpet so that you might walk therein on spacious paths," the Holy Book says (71:19–20), and we have been created in delightful diversity so that we might be intrigued to get to know one another (49:13).

Another way to embrace the mystery and beauty of life is to learn the art of letting go of all that stands in the way of our inner development: for example, a belief that does not serve the common good, an argument that serves no purpose except saving face, a relationship that is toxic, a grudge that depletes our being. By letting go, we release our inner clutter and cultivate inner spaciousness. Most important, we prevent ourselves from being trapped like the monkeys in South Asia, where hunters carve a small hole in a hollow coconut and fill it with fragrant food to entice their prey. The coconut is then tied to a tree. By straightening its fingers the monkey can squeeze its hand into the hole to get the food, but once it clutches the food, its fist is too large to pull out of the hole. The monkey is trapped! It shrieks and jumps up and down hysterically, but never realizes that simply by letting go of the food, it could pull out its hand and escape. How many peculiar situations do we find ourselves in because we cannot let go of our attachments?

 # REFLECTIONS

Travel throughout the Earth and see how Allah originated creation (Qur'an 29:20) ... and the variations in your languages and your colors: verily in that are signs for those who know. (Qur'an 30:22)

O God! Show me things as they really are! (Prayer of the Prophet Muhammad)

Consider, says Rumi, how it is to have a conversation with an embryo. You might talk about the wonders of the world outside the womb: in sunlight, the beauty of orchards in bloom and the joy of friends dancing at a wedding and at nighttime, the countless sparkling of stars and mystery of galaxies. Listen to the answer of the embryo, "There is no other world. I only know what I have experienced. You must be hallucinating!"

Your work is not to search for love but merely to seek and find obstacles within yourself that you have built against it. (Rumi)

 # PRACTICE

What ingrained beliefs do you have that may be harming your soul because they do not serve the common good? Continue to shine the light of awareness on them.

What are some attachments that you need to let go of? Write them down and give yourself permission to look at them. Embrace any feelings that arise, including those that prompt laughter and tears. Choose one attachment and create a tender ritual of releasing it to Spirit. Move on to the next attachment when you are ready. With each successive ritual, it becomes easier and easier to let go.

Fear Is All You Need

A cruel and tyrannical king was curious about the Mulla's reputation as a profound mystic, so he summoned the Mulla and said, "Prove to me that you are a mystic or I'll have you executed." Immediately the Mulla rolled his eyes, stared widely into the skies, and declared, "I see in the mysterious galaxies a monstrously large, birdlike creature with wings so large they could span this entire town, guarding those realms." Then, convulsing and rolling on the ground, he exclaimed, "I see, deep inside the earth, monsters and demons chasing one another." Greatly impressed, the king exclaimed to the Mulla, "How are you able to peer into the unknown?" "Your majesty," replied the Mulla, "fear is all you need!"

A little fear can be a useful thing. Fear of a heart attack can motivate us to watch our diet and get proper exercise, and fear of failing grades can prompt us to hit the books when we'd rather be playing computer games. But too much fear can be a consuming fire. When the sensation of fear grips our being, our imagination runs wild and we become fixated on undesirable outcomes that assume monstrous shapes and grow ever larger if they are not checked, triggering overwhelming feelings of anxiety and panic. A folktale from South Asia speaks to the power of imaginary dangers. A sorcerer goes to a village, mesmerizes all the villagers, and tells them that a ferocious monster is lurking in the village. The villagers cower inside their homes, with doors locked and lights turned off. When they venture outside, they carry weapons and protective gear, and that is how they greet each other: armed and armored, and locked in a trance of fear.

How are we to deal with this kind of fear? Not by buying more locks or weapons, but by breaking the trance, which can only be done by naming our fears and giving ourselves the courage and grace to look at them again and again. Sufi teachers caution us not to dismiss or downplay our imaginary fears, for what we conjure up in the imaginative dimension affects the realm of what we call reality and vice versa. If that sounds abstract or implausible, know that modern psychology agrees that the subconscious does not differentiate between real and imagined, between fact and fiction. Thoughts in the subconscious, especially when infused with feelings, affect our attitudes and behavior in the conscious world. When we are feeling anxious and are conjuring up imaginary fears, it is critical to do some sort of spiritual intervention as early as possible before we become overwhelmed. A little sapling is easy to pull out by the roots, but once it grows into a tree, you will need to call a professional to cut it down.

There are several spiritual practices that can help us tame our fears of invisible monsters. Meditation can calm the mind, positive self-talk can bolster our spirits, and consultation with our authentic community can lead to different perspectives. Above all, there is the practice of faith in something greater than our personalities or human institutions. Call that greater entity God, Creator, Sustainer, Cherisher—whatever terminology speaks to you. Consider that you grew from a sperm in the womb, says Rumi. Did you have any idea what roads you would take before you took them? And yet, here you are. In exactly the same way and with the same mercy, mystery, and providence, we shall be brought to thousands of other worlds.

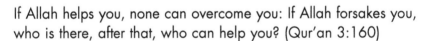

REFLECTIONS

If Allah helps you, none can overcome you: If Allah forsakes you, who is there, after that, who can help you? (Qur'an 3:160)

Those who believe, do deeds of righteousness, and establish regular prayers and regular charity will have their reward with their Lord: on them shall be no fear, nor shall they grieve. (Qur'an 2:277)

How did the rose ever open its heart and give to the world all its beauty? It felt the encouragement of light against its being. Otherwise we all remain too frightened. (Hafiz)

PRACTICE

When you are feeling anxious, a very effective practice is to concentrate on your nostrils and be present with your breath moment to moment. This simple meditation will lower your pulse rate and soften the sharp edge of anxiety.

The moment you realize that negative imaginary scenarios are swirling in your mind and triggering feelings of fear, immediately intervene and tell yourself: "Not real! Not real!" Remind yourself that you are more than your thoughts, more than your fears. Repeat a verse from the Qur'an, "To God we belong and to God we are returning," and tell yourself to trust that all will be well.

Sufi teachers tell us that the feeling of fear in its essence is begging for attention and love from us. With compassion for self, acknowledge the fear, and, little by little, allow yourself to experience and embrace the feeling. Locate the sensations in your body. With tenderness be present with the fear. Perhaps have a little conversation with it, and then release it to Spirit.

If you have a circle of friends and family members you love and trust, share your fears with them. They may offer perspectives and insights that give you comfort and hope.

Fear Has No Favorites

Sufi teachers are emphatic in cautioning us that using exaggerated fear, individually or collectively, to manipulate or convince others will, undoubtedly, result in unhappy consequences. No matter how well intentioned we might be in our use of fear, we are treading on dangerous ground. Fear, as mentioned in the previous chapter, is like fire. When used recklessly it easily gets out of control and consumes all.

A mother brought her young son to the Mulla, complaining that she had tried everything she could think of to convince him to be less rude and rebellious. "Please," she said, "do something to put a little fear in his heart." The Mulla stared fiercely into the boy's eyes and commanded him to listen to his mother. He contorted his face terribly and let out deep growls. He looked and sounded so fearsome that the mother fainted and the Mulla rushed out of the room. When the mother regained consciousness, she berated the Mulla, "I asked you to frighten my son, not me." The Mulla replied, "Madam, when you invoke fear, it consumes everyone. Fear has no favorites. Did you not notice that I myself got so scared that I had to leave the room?"

Using fear habitually to control the behavior of others, no matter how well intentioned, can backfire and be incapacitating. In a Rumi story a mother induces her young son to behave by telling him that if he doesn't, the bogeyman will get him. He grows up with this notion of fear. In his early teens, he has to walk by a graveyard to go to school and is frightened of an imaginary bogeyman following him. When he informs his mother of his fear, she assures him that all he has to do is confront the bogeyman, go right through it, and the bogeyman will evaporate. "Trust me," says the mother. "I know about these things." The son is pensive for a moment and replies, "But what if the bogeyman's mother tells him the same thing? Bogeymen have mothers, too, you know."

REFLECTION

Fear is the cheapest room in the house. I would like to see you living in better conditions. (Hafiz)

PRACTICE

On a piece of paper, make a list of individuals and authorities who have induced fear in you over your lifetime. Awareness is empowerment. In the next step, close your eyes and talk in the imaginal realm to the person or authority that generated the fear in you. With compassion for self and from a place of higher awareness, say whatever your heart desires. End your expression with an affirmation of letting go of your fear and release the person who induced it to the realm of Spirit. In the last step, burn the paper as an act of purification and release.

Make a list of people in your life whom you consciously or unconsciously manipulate through use of fear. Reflect on ways you can minimize the fear tactic and replace it with something more life-affirming.

Wariness of
Religious
Institutions

Deferred Spiritual Maintenance

Just as human beings can go astray when they neglect their inner spiritual work, religious institutions have a tendency to become sterile, corrupt, and dysfunctional when they lapse into what Sufis call "deferred spiritual maintenance." They become more interested in pomp and power and less invested in spirituality and service. They become overly attached to fund-raising and recruitment, and to guard their prerogatives they develop their own sectarian theology and claim exclusive ownership of divine truth.

The Mulla listened one rainy monsoon evening as the clerics at a religious establishment tried to outdo each other in describing the unique beauty and superiority of their religious institution. A fierce storm was brewing and soon the rafters of the sacred house began to sway and creak ominously. "Not to worry," said the head cleric, "These rafters are actually singing hymns of praise out of love for God." The Mulla raised his hand, and, pointing to the wavering rafters, asked, "But what if the rafters, out of love for God, decide to bow and prostrate to Divinity!"

To bolster recruitment and arouse enthusiasm among adherents, religious clerics often make extraordinary promises that certain beliefs and practices will guarantee happiness on earth and a place in the lofty mansions of Heaven. Sadly, many of us are spiritually lazy and willing to believe them. Who wouldn't want to attain Paradise without exertion, freedom without sacrifice, perfection without struggle, riches without work?!

A Mulla story pokes gentle fun at our desire to achieve enlightenment without doing the necessary work. A student came to him and said, "I have heard that there are secret words that, when repeated, open the gates of enlightenment, accelerate our ability to find contentment in life, and connect us to divine mysteries." "Absolutely true!" said the Mulla. "You may start your special secret lessons tomorrow and will be joined by a student who is at a similar level of attainment." The next day the student arrived with eager anticipation and found the Mulla teaching the mystical words to a parrot!

Unscrupulous clerics may claim that their promises of effortless salvation are not far-fetched because the Grace of God will bring them to fruition. But Sufi sages counter that claim by reminding us that this divine blessing, called *baraka* in Islam, is forthcoming only when it is preceded by genuine efforts to become a better human being. In the words of the Qur'an, "The human being can have nothing except that for which he strives" (53:39).

Thus it behooves us to select our spiritual teachers with care. Clerical ordination is not necessary for a person to be a genuine spiritual teacher, and ordination in itself does not confer the grace of enlightened leadership. The Qur'an says there is no need for an intermediary between us and God, and Islam theoretically does not espouse ordination at all. "Every Muslim is his own priest," said the Prophet Muhammad. Another time he said, "The only priest you need is awareness of your own death." When we are truly conscious of our death, priorities quickly rearrange themselves and we make sound decisions with no need for clerical guidance.

In practice, some Sunni and Shia denominations of Islam are now controlled by clerics who have assumed political and religious power and have created hierarchies that have little to do with authentic spirituality. The Mulla is consistently critical of their role in corrupting the religious institutions by serving temporal power and neglecting the spiritual message. In a typical story, the Mulla noticed the devil sitting down, looking confident and relaxed. "Why are you just sitting there, making no mischief?" the Mulla asked. Replied the devil, "Since the clerics, theoreticians, and would-be teachers of the religious paths have appeared in such numbers, there is nothing left for me to do."

REFLECTIONS

The most ignorant among you is the one who does not learn from changes in the world. (*Hadith*)

Three agents destroy religion: an ill-tempered scholar, a tyrannical leader, and an ignorant theologian. (*Hadith*)

You may follow one stream. Realize that it leads to the Ocean. Do not mistake the stream for the Ocean. (Jan Fishman)[1]

If the relationship between me and my religion gets in the way of my relationship with you, it will surely get in the way of my relationship with God. (Traditional saying)

A progressive contemporary scholar of religion asks us to beware of the following warning signs in religious institutions:

> They claim to have the absolute truth.
>
> They demand blind obedience.
>
> They preach that the end is coming at a specific time.
>
> They believe that their cause justifies any means.
>
> They declare "Holy War" on unbelievers.[2]

PRACTICE

What are some issues you have with institutional religion? Do you feel safe and comfortable talking about them? Whom do you talk to?

Do you ever find yourself in a position where you defend the pronouncements of your religious institution, even though you have strong doubts about it? How do you deal with that?

What are some aspects of institutional religion you respect?

How Some Religious Customs Began

The Mulla was bowing to God during daily prayers in the mosque, when his shirt came untucked and exposed his back in an unseemly fashion. Trying to be of help, the man behind him pulled on the shirt to lower it. Immediately the Mulla pulled on the shirt of the man in front of him, and thus began a chain reaction that has become a tradition during public prayer. Absurdly, at some point a cleric felt the need for authorization of this time-honored practice, and in due course an appropriate *hadith* was fabricated.

This story is a prime example of how easily some traditions can be established and how difficult it is to uproot them once they have acquired "legitimacy" with the passage of time. The shirt-pulling practice is harmless and amusing, but other, more harmful practices have taken root because of believers' uncritical and unquestioning acceptance of traditions that were created for the convenience of all-too-human leaders in the vacuum of deferred spiritual maintenance. In Islam, most of these harmful traditions are supported by fabricated *hadith*, which purport to claim that the Prophet himself advocated them.

The consequences are tragic for Muslim women in some parts of the world, where false accusations of adultery or fornication can result in their death by stoning, even though there is no verse in the Qur'an that sanctions this barbarous practice. It is enough for some Muslims that the Prophet is said to have authorized it, and they believe the lie with all their hearts. The Prophet, foreseeing the harm that could be done falsely in his name, pronounced that no *hadith* ascribed to him is to be deemed valid if it runs counter to the spirit of the Qur'an. The *hadith* claiming that the Prophet sentenced adulterous women to be stoned to death have been discredited by serious scholars, but some imams draw attention to a mind-boggling story related by an otherwise respected *hadith* compiler, Sunan Ibn Majah. According to this story, the Prophet received a verse on stoning and entrusted it to his wife Aisha, who kept the paper on which it was written under her pillow. Why was the paper never found and published? Because the Prophet fell ill, and in the ensuing chaos, a goat entered the room and ate the paper!

Another set of concocted and contradictory *hadith* forbids women to visit gravesites, supposedly because the sight of women weeping in the cemetery is sexually stimulating for men. Scholars who have examined this issue explain that in pre-Islamic seventh-century Arabia, it was a local custom to hire professional women to attend funerals and cry hysterically, clutch their hair, and thump their chests to indicate unbearable grief. It was this specific practice that the Prophet discouraged, not the presence of genuinely grieving widows, daughters, and other female relatives, and female friends.

Another injunction supposedly based on *hadith* says that music is forbidden in Islam. This is laughable because anyone who has visited Muslim countries knows that music is an integral part of Islamic culture. The language of the Qur'an is musical in its very nature. Music echoes the sounds of the cosmos, and our souls love it because those moments of treble and bass evoke the universal harmony of which they were a part long before our current birth.

The Sufi sage Rumi extolled the sacred beauty and majesty of music and often led his congregants in religious chants and songs all night long. One night a conservative practitioner joined the congregation but became so uncomfortable with the singing, music, and drumming that he finally burst out in protest, "What is all this singing and singing?!" Rumi replied, "It's the sound of the creaking of the doors of Paradise." "Well I hate the sound of creaking," cried the outraged man. Rumi answered back, "That's because when you hear the sound of creaking, for you the doors of Paradise are closing!"

Sufi teachers are adamant and unambiguous about the following guidance: No matter how time-honored a tradition may be, no matter how loud the claims that it is sacred and authentic, if it does not serve the common good and causes suffering while in no way contributing to spiritual healing, it must be taken out of circulation and radically reexamined with an open mind and heart.

REFLECTIONS

We shall not take human beings for our lords besides God.
(Qur'an 3:64)

This religion is easy. No one becomes harsh and strict in the
religion without it overwhelming him. So, fulfill your duties as best
as you can and rejoice. Rely upon the efforts of the morning and
the evening and a little at night and you will reach your goal.
(*Hadith*)

PRACTICE

What are some religious traditions or customs that you are
uncomfortable with? How do you deal with your objections?

What are some religious customs, traditions, and requirements
that you feel are prejudicial and harmful? Make a list, and commit
yourself to removing them from your life.

Every season, or during religious festivities, renew your
commitment to a religious custom that is loving, healing, and
serves the common good.

Belief, Faith, and Borrowed Certainty

Many of our religious beliefs are based on hearsay. They do not emerge from within us but are rooted in what teachers call "borrowed certainty." We borrow from someone else's beliefs and experiences.

A friend brought the Mulla a few ducks he had hunted in the wild. Together, they prepared a large pot of delicious duck soup and enjoyed a hearty meal. The next day, the Mulla received a visitor who introduced himself as a "friend of the friend who brought you the ducks." The Mulla happily fed him duck soup. In the following days, more visitors arrived, calling themselves "friends of the friend of the friend who gifted you the ducks." The Mulla graciously fed them duck soup. But then came another visitor who claimed to be a "friend of the friend of the friend of the friend." By this time, the Mulla was annoyed. He seated the guest and brought him a bowl of hot water. Eagerly, the guest tasted the soup, and then exclaimed in disappointment, "What is this? This is no duck soup." "Yes, it is," exclaimed the Mulla, "This is the soup of the soup of the soup of the duck!"

Mere tepid adherence to a watered-down "soup of the soup" version of religious beliefs is not enough to achieve fulfillment in this world or the next. The Qur'an urges us in several verses (e.g., 102:5, 102:7, 69:51) to go through three stages in order to get past hearsay and arrive at inner knowing through our own personal experience. Sufi teachers also encourage us to question religious beliefs and adopt only those that nurture and support our deep inner faith.

I still remember my own experience as an eleven-year-old child questioning the stories that were taught in religion class. Our teacher, who doubled as a science teacher, regaled us with Qur'anic stories about survival in the belly of a whale, turning a rod into a serpent, parting the Red Sea, turning a lump of clay into a bird, flying through the cosmos at night, conceiving a child at a ripe age, and the virgin birth. The stories were fascinating but also fantastic, and we naturally asked how we could reconcile them with science. To our surprise and bewilderment, the teacher abruptly ordered us not to question anything in the Holy Book, and that was the end of the discussion. Fortunately, my loving parents provided answers filled with wisdom and metaphors, and encouraged me to ask questions and develop my own understanding.

The absurdity of adamant attachment to religious stories and beliefs was on full display at an interfaith conference some years ago, when Muslim, Christian, and Jewish participants were sharing stories from their traditions about Abraham, Ismail, Isaac, Sarah, Hagar and Moses. A number of stories are basically the same in both the Bible and the Qur'an, although they may differ in the details. As we know, the devil is in the details, and the devil at this conference was having a good time fanning the flames of argument and ownership. Voices rose, egos were bruised, and observers fidgeted in embarrassment. Finally, a Native American professor burst out laughing and said, "You know, we Native Americans also have stories. The only difference between us is that you guys believe the stories!"

Someone asked the Mulla, "According to Islamic theology, which is more useful, the Sun or the Moon?" "The answer is obvious," replied the Mulla. "We have plenty of light during the day, so the Sun is not necessary. But it's dark at night, so we need the radiance of the Moon. Therefore, the Moon is far more important than the Sun." With this and several other similarly ridiculous pronouncements, the Mulla teaches us how absurd it is to accept beliefs simply on the say-so of religious authorities. Transforming our beliefs into a deep inner knowing is a lifelong task, which we can accomplish only by consulting our hearts and minds and learning from personal experience.

 REFLECTIONS

The three stages of belief in the Qur'an are as follows:

> *ilm ul yaqin,* or belief based on hearsay knowledge
> (102:5)
>
> *ayn ul yaqin,* or belief based on personal witnessing
> (102:7)

haq ul yaqin, or belief based on inner experience of truth (69:51)

He it is who has bestowed upon thee from on high this divine writ ... but none save God knows its final meaning ... none takes this to heart save those who are endowed with insight. (Qur'an 3:7)

O my Sustainer! Open for me my heart! (Qur'an 20:25)

O my Sustainer, increase me in knowledge! (Qur'an 20:114)

How ugly rings the metallic music of their rigidities and certainties! (Rumi, speaking about those who are stuck at the level of hearsay and unthinking belief).

PRACTICE

Do you espouse any religious beliefs that are rooted not in your personal conviction but in hearsay and "borrowed certainty"? Make a list of them and spend some time reflecting on how they resonate in your heart. Become aware of how your reflections affect your attitudes and behavior.

Share some religious beliefs that have arisen from your own personal and life experiences.

Create or join a group in which you feel safe and comfortable in discussing your hesitation about certain beliefs. Seek and share counsel from members on how you can build faith in those beliefs that ring true for you.

Spiritual
Practices

Honor the Present Moment

"By the essence of time," says the Qur'an, "verily, all humankind is in deep loss except those who believe in the oneness of Allah and perform good works and remind each other of the truth" (103:1–3). And the essence of time, according to spiritual teachers of all traditions, is the present moment. "Now" is all we have, and yet we squander this precious moment by allowing our minds to flit back and forth between regrets about the past and anxieties about the future. Our mind sways back and forth, but it is in our power to discipline it gently and gradually to be more focused on the present moment, to be more aware of the oneness of creation in each moment so that our works are good and our words are true. Only in the now is there fullness and fulfillment.

If we are unmindful of the divine qualities flowing through the present moment, nothing we have accomplished or acquired will please or satisfy us. One day the Mulla met a man who was wandering the world, with all his belongings in a single knapsack, in search of happiness. So far, he complained, nothing in life had given him joy or contentment. Suddenly, the Mulla seized the knapsack and ran down the road. "Stop!" yelled the man. "Those are my life possessions!" The Mulla easily outran the man and then, at a curve in the road, dropped the bag and waited in concealment. The seeker shouted with joy and relief upon discovering his possessions. The Mulla came out of his hiding place and said, "Before you get angry, notice that you feel happy now. You were not present with the joy of your belongings until you lost them. May you learn to cherish what you have!"

To reemphasize this critical insight of not taking the blessings in our life for granted, Sufi teachers like to relate the following story. One day the Mulla's donkey disappeared. The Mulla promptly announced an award to anyone who found his lost donkey. The reward was ... his donkey! "Are you crazy?" his family and friends remarked. "Not at all," replied the Mulla. "You do not understand that the joy of recovering what is lost is greater than the joy of possessing it!"

It is wise to meditate on a timeless Sufi insight: "A Sufi is a son or daughter of the present moment." This insight brought midnight relief to a ninth-century Muslim commander who had been captured and thrown into prison. Beside himself with anxiety and fear, he was unable to sleep because he was certain he would be tortured and killed the next day. But then, deep inside, he heard the words of his Sufi teacher: "A Sufi is a son of the present moment." At that moment he realized that his fearful thoughts about the next day were merely thoughts, not real. Only the present moment was real, and with that realization he was able to fall asleep. Morning came and instead of being killed, he was exchanged for a prisoner from the opposing side. For us, too, a more hopeful morning dawns when we repeat that Sufi mantra and open ourselves to the truth that only the present moment is real.

To be in the present moment does not mean that we simply ignore past or future events. Of course we need to learn from our experiences and plan for what lies ahead. Rather, it means that we should be conscious of our thoughts and give ourselves permission to spend a certain amount of intentional time in the past or future. It could be as simple as telling oneself, "I give myself permission to spend the next twenty minutes feeling my regrets of the past and learning from them" or "I give myself twenty minutes to feel anxiety about this future possibility and make necessary plans." In this way we honor the present moment, and by setting a time limit we guard ourselves against sliding into the morass of unconscious anxiety, overcome by the demons of fear and regret.

We know from our own lives how important it is to pay attention to the present moment, and how costly it can be when we don't. We have all had accidents (hopefully, only minor) caused by a moment of inattention: stubbed toes, sprained ankles, spilled milk, burned cookies.

The Mulla wasn't paying attention when he went to the market to purchase flour and salt. "Make sure not to mix the two," cautioned his wife. The shopkeeper filled his dish with flour and after he measured the salt, the Mulla turned the plate over to provide a separate place for the salt. The flour fell to the floor but the salt was safe. When he returned home, his wife asked, "Where's the flour?" "Right here," said the Mulla, turning the plate over and dropping the salt to the floor. Truly, the Mulla lost his flour and salt due to his inattention, just as we lose the blessings of the moment when we allow ourselves to sleepwalk unconsciously through our precious days.

 # REFLECTIONS

Useless is a wonderful milk yield from a cow that kicks the pail over.[1] (Hazrat Muinuddin Chisti)

Those who are unmindful have "hearts with which they fail to grasp the truth and eyes with which they fail to see and ears with which they fail to hear." (Qur'an 7:179)

If you become addicted to looking back, half your life will be spent in distraction and the other half in regret. (Rumi)

Make everything in you an ear, each atom of your being, and you will hear at every moment what the Source is whispering to you. (Rumi)

 # PRACTICE

Make a list of the blessings of people, situations, and possessions in your life that you take for granted. In what ways can you be more present with them?

One of the best ways to be present is to train yourself to listen deeply. Listen with your heart. Focus on your physical heart when others are speaking and also when you yourself are saying something. The person who is continuously present with his or her heart when someone speaks will metaphorically begin to hear what Rumi calls "birdsong in the egg." Listening from the heart to your own words will make you aware of the wisdom of Hazrat Ali that words are under your control until you have spoken them, but you are under their control once you have spoken them.

What are some sad or angry incidents from your past that you revisit often? Become aware of how this reliving of the memory and feelings affects you. Can you remind yourself that a true human being is a son or daughter of the present moment?

Think of one intense worry you have about the future. Give yourself a specific amount of time to allow yourself to consciously experience the anxiety and make a plan for the future.

With eyes closed, allow yourself to feel a nagging regret or anxiety. With mercy for yourself, embrace it with your consciousness. Be present with this feeling. Then, imagine yourself releasing it to Spirit. You might say to it, "I surrender you to Spirit." Use words that conform to your belief system. Follow this with one of the meditations listed below.

Try one or more of the following meditative practices to become grounded, centered, and present:

> Close your eyes and focus on your nostrils. Be present with your breath as you inhale and exhale. Continue for several minutes.

> Close your eyes and bring your attention to rest on your heart. Place your hand over your heart and for a time listen to your heart beat. Feel the rhythm of your heartbeat in the palm of your hand.

> With your eyes closed, focus on the lowest part of your spine and intentionally send a chord of divine light from there deep into the Earth. Feel a connection to the womb of Mother Earth. Focus next on the crown of your head and intentionally send a chord of divine light upward, piercing the mysterious realms and connecting you to the heart of Heaven. Repeat several times and then stay poised between Heaven and Earth.

Strive to Be Grateful

"All that is in the Heavens and all that is on earth extolls the limitless glory of God," says the Qur'an (62:1). When we raise our voices in praise and thanksgiving, we join that cosmic chorus and our personalities become aligned with a universal vibration. We participate in life's greatest mystery: the relationship of creation to Creator.

Even in times of pain and loss, the Sufi way is to be grateful for blessings that we may not be able to recognize at the moment.

One day the Mulla discovered that his donkey—his helper, companion, and source of livelihood—had disappeared. The entire village searched far and wide, but to no avail. The donkey was simply gone. In the evening, the villagers found the Mulla on his knees in the town square, raising his hands toward Heaven and exclaiming, "Thank you, Allah! Thank you, Allah!" "Mulla," they asked, don't you realize that your donkey is lost forever?" "I know, I know," replied the Mulla. "But I have so much to be grateful for. Imagine what could have happened to me if I had been on the donkey!"

Despite our attempts to live as consciously as possible, we take countless things for granted and don't even think to be grateful for them. "Which of your Lord's blessings will you deny?" asks the Qur'an repeatedly in chapter fifty-five. We don't really deny the blessings; we just don't notice them until something makes us aware. We don't realize that life is full of nontoothache moments or non-mosquito-bite moments until we break a tooth or experience itching that keeps us awake at night. The ninth-century Sufi sage Rabia once met a young man who was walking around with his head bound in a towel and bemoaning his terrible headache to anyone who would listen. After expressing appropriate concern, she asked if he had ever experienced moments of good health. "Oh yes, for most of my life," replied the man. "And in those moments," Rabia asked pointedly, "did you ever wear a colored turban and jump up and down in celebration?"

When we practice gratitude in happy times, we create a sacred vibration that can sustain us in difficult moments. This is certainly the case in my motherland, Bangladesh. According to the Happy Planet Index, Bangladesh consistently ranks among the happiest countries in the world, even though it is severely overcrowded, impoverished, and visited frequently by natural disasters. How can people be happy in such conditions? I believe it is because Bangladeshis are grateful people, praising God and celebrating when times are good. This practice of gratitude helps them cope with difficulties that would overwhelm most of us who are used to our American comforts. In a BBC report in 2009, a Bangladeshi professor described the squalor of the flood-ravaged slum through which she passed on her way to and from her upper-class neighborhood. With their homes destroyed, people were living in makeshift tarpaulin tents on the pavement. "I would be the one grumbling about the rising floodwaters lapping at our car," she said, "while the squatters took time to live, laugh, and enjoy … someone would play the flute, children would sing and dance and everyone would celebrate just being alive.... They certainly taught me a thing or two about human resilience."[2]

If we are truly resilient, we may even find blessings embedded in our misfortunes. The Sufis have a saying: "Beneath every ruin is a treasure." Every event—good or bad—is part of a larger story and plays a part in making us who we are. Thus, a useful prayer in a difficult situation is this: "O God, save me from its harm but please do not deprive me of its good." It is critical to remember, however, that hidden pearls become real only when they emerge from our personal experience and realization. It would be a serious injustice and disservice to tell others to find hidden blessings in the midst of their suffering.

We humans tend to expect good things in life as if that were our due. But, as the Qur'an says, "Now let man but think from what he is created" (86:5), reminding us that we are little more than lumps of clay and dust. Sufis like to tell the story of Ayaz, who exemplified the spirit of that Qur'anic admonition. Starting as a lowly slave, Ayaz rose to a high position in the tenth-century court of the powerful Sultan Mahmud of Ghaznavi. Every day for the rest of his life, Ayaz retired to a secret chamber where he took off his robes and put on the rags he had worn as a slave. Then, contemplating his lowly self in a mirror, he gave thanks for his miraculous good fortune and prayed never to forget the blessings of God.

We too would do well to reflect frequently on our origins and divine blessings, starting with the gift of life itself. A favorite Sufi practice is to express gratitude several times a day with the words, "O God, favor upon favor have You bestowed upon this handful of dust." With the regular practice of gratitude, over time we will experience joy, peace, and fulfillment no matter what our station and circumstances may be.

REFLECTIONS

Remember with gratitude the blessings that God has bestowed upon you. (Qur'an 3:103)

Anyone who gives thanks does so to the profit of his own soul. (Qur'an 31:12)

Gratitude for the abundance you have received is the best insurance that the abundance will continue. (*Hadith*)

For sixty years I have been forgetful, every minute, but not for a second has this flowing toward me stopped or slowed. (Rumi)

I saw grief drinking a cup of sorrow and said to it, "Tastes sweet, does it not?" Grief confessed, "You've caught me and ruined my business. How can I sell sorrow when you know it's a blessing?" (Rumi)

When one continues to give thanks in times of affliction, one is giving thanks for unknown blessings already on their way. (Traditional Sufi saying)

Ayesha, wife of the Prophet Muhammad, reported that when the Prophet saw what pleased him, he said, "Praise be to God whose grace brings all goodness to perfection." If he saw what he disliked, he said, "Praise be to God under all conditions."

PRACTICE

What are some hidden blessings from a difficult period of your life that have emerged from your own experience? How has that discernment changed your understanding of suffering?

What are some blessings you are thankful for in the course of your daily life? Make a list. Create a ritual of gratitude before sleeping. If you do this daily, Sufi teachers say that you are creating feathers and wings to the bird of Spirit within you.

Sufis make it a habit to touch their heart whenever they express thanks to someone. Over time the practice becomes natural and practitioners report feeling a sense of wholeness, inner peace, and sacred joy.

When someone gives you a gift, thank the giver, but also remember to thank the Giver. If someone presents you with a beautiful hat, you need to express thanks to the person who gave it to you. But shouldn't you also be grateful to the Giver who gave you the head on which the hat will dwell?

Spirit of Prayer

The Mulla was languishing in jail and hoping that his teacher would slip him a weapon or some other means of escape when he came to visit. But what the teacher brought was a prayer rug, which he presented with the advice to pray fervently and regularly. "What a useless present," the Mulla thought, but with nothing else to do all day he reluctantly began to bow and prostrate himself to God in the Islamic manner. Despite his initial lack of enthusiasm, he began to feel a strange peace descend on him as the weeks and months rolled by. And then one day it dawned on him: The unusual design woven into the prayer rug was an escape route out of the prison!

Among the many insights to be gleaned from this story is that one prostration to God frees us from a thousand prostrations to our ego. Another is that daily prayer helps us recognize the invisible hand of God shaping the design of our lives. God "always prepares a way of emergence" in ways we could never imagine, says the Qur'an (65:2–3), but to find that way of emergence we need to pray and meditate regularly on our metaphorical prayer rug.

The Mulla's prostrations are the traditional manner of Islamic prayer, which the Prophet imparted to his followers after his legendary night journey known as the *miraj*. Astride a mystical steed called Barak, Muhammad was transported from Mecca to the highest hilltop in Jerusalem, from whence he ascended into seven levels of Heaven. Along the way he was dazzled by the sight of luminous angels bowing and prostrating themselves to God as they poured out words of exquisite praise and gratitude. Inspired by that vision, the Prophet urged his followers to imitate the angels by using the gift of their bodies to express adoration of God.

The Prophet also taught that real prayer is more than the distracted performance of bodily prostrations and rote repetition of holy words. Prayer is pointless unless it is done with mindfulness. "So grief to the worshippers who do not pray with their hearts!" says the Qur'an (107:4–5). When asked what is better than prayer, Muhammad answered, "The spirit of prayer." Another time he said, "Worship as if you can see God, and if you cannot see God, know that God sees you."

The Mulla was obviously familiar with the Prophet's teachings, for he had a perfect riposte for a self-righteous cleric who thought to chide him on the outward form of his midday prayers. Running late with appointments but eager not to skip the appointed time for prayer, the Mulla rushed to a nearby mosque and hurriedly performed his bodily prostrations. The head imam was displeased to see the Mulla's haste and sternly ordered him to repeat his prostrations slowly and deliberately. "Now, don't you think that God will accept this set of prayers?" "Not really," replied the Mulla. "This set of prayers I did for you, but the last one was for God."

On this same theme of mindful prayer, Sufis like to tell a true story about the powerful seventeenth-century Muslim emperor, Akbar of India, who was performing the ritual prayer in a forest when a young peasant woman arrived out of nowhere and walked heedlessly across his path. The emperor was furious at the interruption. "How dare you cross my prayer path?" he yelled as the guards seized her. Trembling with fear and with eyes lowered, she explained that she had not seen the emperor because she was lost in thought about her beloved husband. Then, daring to look at the emperor, she asked how it was possible for him to see her if he also was lost in remembrance of his Beloved. Rather than being affronted by her question, Emperor Akbar was so moved that he gave her a handsome reward for teaching him a valuable lesson about mindfulness in prayer.

REFLECTIONS

Bow in adoration and draw closer. (Qur'an 96:19)

Establish regular prayer: for prayer restrains from shameful and unjust deeds, and remembrance of God is surely the greatest of all things in life. (Qur'an 29:45)

Celebrate God's praises, and do this often; and glorify Him morning and evening. (Qur'an 33:42)

PRACTICE

What practices do you do to remain conscious of Divinity or Spirit daily? Set aside some regular times every day to connect with the Unknown. It could be through meditation, silence, or ritual prayer. Be realistic in your allocation of time. Create and build your daily schedule around times you have apportioned for connecting with Spirit and not the other way around. In other words, don't plan to meditate or pray only when you get time in your busy schedule. You will never find the time unless it is a true priority.

Efficacy of Prayers of Supplication

"Thee do we beseech for help," Muslims pray several times a day when they recite *Al-Fatiha*, the opening chapter of the Qur'an. Supplications are an integral part of Islamic prayer, and God assures us that "I listen to the prayer of every supplicant" (Qur'an 2:186). But we humans are inclined to be hasty, cautions the Holy Book: "Human beings often pray for things that are harmful as if they were praying for that which is good." (17:11)

The Mulla's prayers for his two daughters are a good example of how complicated and contradictory our prayers may be. The daughters lived in different neighborhoods of the same town. One was married to a brick maker and wanted the Mulla to pray for sunshine because they had fired the kiln and baked some bricks. The other daughter begged him to pray for rain because she and her husband had just sown seeds. So the Mulla prayed for sunshine to bless only the east side of town and for rain to fall gently on the west side of town. And, he added, if God got the exact boundaries of east and west mixed up, could He please shower the Mulla with some gold coins so that he could compensate his daughters for God's mistake?

Rather than only pleading for material blessings, it is worthwhile for us to make supplications that bring us closer to God. The Prophet used to pray, "O God, grace me with love of You and to love those who love You and to love whatever brings me nearer to You."

Whatever your supplications may be, state them clearly and sincerely. Don't come from a place of rote supplication. That routine warbling of words does not reflect any great need for divine intervention. Plead from the depths of your soul with what Sufis call "increased necessity." We receive divine blessing according to our need, so Rumi advises us to increase our need so that the "Sea of Abundance may surge up in loving-kindness." Have you not noticed, he asks, that only when a baby is born do a mother's breasts become filled with milk in response to increased need for that wondrous, life-sustaining nutrition?

Do prayers of supplication really work? Someone asked the Prophet that question, pointing out that everything seems to be predetermined and preordained, so what good is prayer? Replied the Prophet, "The reversal of misfortune by means of petition and weeping is also part of the preordained decree."

It is unwise to assume that we know better than God what is good for us or what will move the divine Heart on our account. One more Mulla story illustrates the point. The education minister brought the village children to the mosque one day during a drought, claiming that the cries of the innocent would certainly move the heart of God. "It's not the cries—innocent or criminal—that count," declared the Mulla, "but wisdom and awareness." "Prove your point," shouted the minister, "or you will be denounced as a heretic for your blasphemous statements." "That's simple," said the Mulla. "If the prayers of innocent children counted, there would be no school for you to administer, for children generally dislike going to school." He added, "If you have survived those prayers and have a job today, it is because of the prayers of some adults who know better than the children what is good for them."

REFLECTIONS

Call to your Sustainer humbly and in the secrecy of your hearts. (Qur'an 7:55)

Bestow upon us the gift of Your grace: truly You are the Giver of Gifts. (Qur'an 3:8)

PRACTICE

What are some of your personal supplications? Place them in your heart with intention and mindfulness. Place your hands over your heart and plead with Divinity for their fruition. Add the sentence, "This or whatever is in my highest interest is manifesting for me now." End by summoning and feeling gratitude for blessings already received and those that are on their way.

Efficacy of Rituals
and Spiritual Practices

How effective are religious rituals and spiritual practices? Very effective, according to the Mulla, who performed a peculiar ritual every evening at 5 P.M. sharp. Sitting under a particular tree in his garden, he whistled a tune, mumbled some words aloud, raised his arms to the Heavens, then lowered his hands, closed his eyes, and sat in silence for about twenty minutes. He concluded the ritual by spreading breadcrumbs on his flowerbeds. Eventually, his neighbor asked if he did this to make his plants flourish. "No," replied the Mulla, "I do it to keep away ferocious tigers and wolves." "But Mulla," said the neighbor, "there are no tigers and wolves for thousands of miles." "I know," said the Mulla. "Effective, isn't it?"

What makes a spiritual practice or ritual effective? No one knows for sure. The elements of faith and purity of heart surely play a role, but spiritual teachers agree that it is critical to be as fully engaged with our practices as we are with our prayers. The moment we lapse into rote repetition of a practice, it loses its efficacy.

A highly recommended spiritual practice is any activity that brings us into frequent contact with reminders of the impermanence and fragility of life. The Prophet Muhammad urged his followers to visit the sick, help prepare the deceased for burial, attend funerals, and pray at gravesites in order to grow in the wisdom and compassion to be gained from consciousness of one's mortality. But the Mulla reminds us that we don't earn spiritual benefits simply by doing the deeds without attention and intentionality. "Notice," he says, "that not all health practitioners or funeral directors are sages or saints!"

Among Sufis, a favorite spiritual practice is *zihr,* the chanting of divine praise or other sacred mantras. These chanting sessions, especially in a circle of sincere fellow chanters, can produce states of ecstasy and remembrance that infuse our daily lives with joy and allow us to taste the sweetness that Rumi describes as existing before honey or bee. By repeating sacred mantras in a heartfelt way, whether in a group or on our own, we dip our beings in God-consciousness. Eventually, through a process similar to dipping fabric repeatedly in a vat of dye, our souls become infused with divine beauty.

Finally, yet another favorite Sufi practice is mindful silence—not the absence of sound, but of the little self. When we silence the chatter of the ego, even for a few brief moments, we are able to commune with the Mystery and grow in awareness and peace.

REFLECTIONS

Our life takes its hue from God! And who could give a better hue to life than God, if we truly worship Him? (Qur'an 2:138)

Thy Sustainer's greatness glorify! (Qur'an 74:3). Render your innermost hearts free of all dross. (Qur'an 3:154)

An hour of contemplation is better than a year of prayer. (*Hadith*)

When we praise God, God does not become holy; we become holy. (Traditional Sufi saying)

Silence is the language of God. Everything else is a poor translation. (Rumi)

PRACTICE

What are some spiritual practices you do daily? If you don't have any, adopt at least one or two that are simple and have enough appeal that you will do them daily. For example, touch your heart as often as possible during the day and silently say "thank you" for the blessings that come your way. Remember to do them mindfully if you want to obtain the greatest benefit.

Signs in Nature

One of the best ways to grow in spiritual wisdom is to reflect on divine signs in nature. More than seven hundred verses of the Qur'an extol those natural signs. "Assuredly, the creation of the Heavens and the Earth is a greater [matter] than the creation of men," says the Qur'an (40:57), and "You will not see any flaws in what the Lord of Mercy creates" (67:3). Therefore, the Holy Book advises, do not walk upon the Earth with proud self-conceit, "for truly, you can never rend the Earth asunder, nor can you grow as tall as the mountains!" (17:37). Instead, we must honor and respect the natural world out of love and awe for its Creator, for "Most Gracious are those who walk on the Earth in humility" (25:63).

Determined to learn wisdom from nature, the Mulla reclined under a huge mulberry tree and surveyed the landscape in front of him. After a while he had an exciting insight and called out to God: "Beloved Creator, something is not symmetrical in Your grand design. I see weak and fragile creepers that grow huge watermelons, and a large mulberry tree that bears the tiniest of berries. Dear Allah, please know that I offer this not in the spirit of criticism but out of a desire to learn from signs in nature. Indeed, divine or human, there is room for improvement for all of us." At that very instant, a tiny berry from the high branches landed on his head, and the Mulla was graced by a deeper insight. "I see! I see!" he exclaimed. "What if the berry had been a watermelon?! Indeed, let me reflect further!"

Perhaps the most frequently cited natural phenomenon in Islamic spirituality is water, which is employed as a metaphor for the power, beauty, and majesty of divine compassion for self and others. There is nothing as soft and yielding as water, yet for overcoming the hardest element there is nothing as powerful as water. Thus, the person who is merciful and gentle is possessed of authentic strength. The Qur'an offers another insight: Water gives life to everything of the created world. In several verses, the Holy Book explains metaphorically that the Earth was parched but when the waters of mercy graced the land, the Earth became "clothed in green" (Qur'an 22:63). The person who is compassionate is also life-giving and life-affirming.

Other metaphors abound in the Qur'an. Trees are mentioned at least twenty-six times in the Holy Book. Describing the value of truth, the Qur'an says it is "like a good tree, firmly rooted, reaching its branches toward the sky, always yielding fruit, by consent of its Sustainer" (14:24–25). For Sufis the tree is an excellent metaphor for unity in diversity: Its branches sway differently in the wind, but all are connected at the roots. And Rumi uses the tree as a metaphor for the lifetime journey from attachment to surrender: The world is like a tree and we humans are the half-ripe fruit upon it. Unripe fruit clings tight to the branch because, immature, it's not yet ready for the palate.

A central Qur'anic metaphor for divine wisdom is the order and balance of the universe in which the Earth rotates faithfully every day. "The Sun is not permitted to overtake the Moon nor can the night go beyond the day, but each moves easily in its lawful way" (Qur'an 36:40). The Sufi poet Hafiz extends the metaphor to describe the eternal love of our Creator. The Earth would die if the Sun stopped kissing her, he says. "Even after all this time, the Sun never tells the Earth, 'Hey, you owe me!' Look what happens with a love like that," says Hafiz: "It lights up the entire sky."

REFLECTIONS

Behold! In the creation of the Heavens and the Earth; in the alternation of the night and day; in the sailing of the ships through the ocean for the profit of humankind; in the rain which Allah sends down from the skies, and the life which He gives therewith to an Earth that is dead: In the beasts of all kinds that He scatters through the earth; in the change of the winds, and the clouds which they trail like their slaves between the sky and the Earth—[here] indeed are signs for a people who are wise. (Qur'an 2:164)

Even if you fear that the Last Day has arrived, plant the sapling you hold in your hand. (*Hadith*)

Grass agrees to die and rise up again so that it can receive a little of the animal's enthusiasm. (Rumi)

PRACTICE

What are some teachings and insights from signs in nature that are especially meaningful for you?

In times of pain and suffering, spend time in nature, which Sufis believe has been graced with divine energies to absorb and transform human suffering. Silently, with feeling, ask nature to help you, and open your heart to experience peace and healing.

Wisdom for
the İnner
Journey

Seeking in the Right Direction

We know from many aspects of our lives that our efforts bear fruit when we exert them in the right direction. The same holds true in our spiritual endeavors: We cannot expect to achieve healing and transformation if we flail about in all directions, mindless of the source of our pain or its solution. A popular Sufi story from the ninth century underlines this crucial point.

The Mulla was looking for a lost key one night under a light atop a pillar in the dark street. Friends joined in the search, without success, until finally someone asked him, "Where approximately do you think you lost the key? I ask so we can better focus our search." To their surprise, the Mulla replied that actually he lost the key inside his house. "Then why search for it here?" they asked in amazement." "That's simple," answered the Mulla. "There is no light in my house, but there is so much light out here."

We laugh, but how often do we do the very same thing? Why is it that when we lose our happiness and peace of mind because of difficulties in a relationship, a job, or income flow, we look for what was lost in external things, rather than in our own hearts? Of course those external difficulties are real and deserve our attention, but they are not the true source of our unhappiness. Instead of spending all our time and energy blaming and trying to fix what is on the outside, we need to focus on the shadows within. That is where we will find and repair what is missing in our spiritual well-being. The work is difficult, but when all is well inside, we will be able to bear life's problems with much more equanimity and awareness.

An important aspect of inner work is to honor and heal our difficult feelings. All feelings are sacred. If our uncomfortable feelings have a sharp edge, it is because they are separated from us and are begging for our attention and love. It is essential to attend to our feelings. Thus, for example, if we want to take the sacred step of forgiving someone who has wronged us, it is absolutely vital to go through the process of healing the pain or anger we feel inside. Otherwise, the outward act of forgiveness remains incomplete and unfulfilled.

Learning to embrace our negative feelings is hard work. No one enjoys feelings of pain and suffering, but embracing and integrating them is the only way to transform the wounded ego into its higher self. Rumi tells a metaphorical story about a man who wanted a heroic lion tattooed on his shoulders. As soon as the needle began to prick, the man howled in pain and asked, "Which part of the lion are you working on?" Informed that it was the tail, the man said he preferred a lion without a tail. So the tattoo artist began working on the lion's ears, but again feeling the pain, the man said, "No ears." No matter which part of the lion the artist tried to draw with his needle, the customer complained. Needless to say, the heroic lion was never completed.

 # REFLECTIONS

God will not change the condition of a people unless they change their inner selves. (Qur'an 13:11)

If you get irritated by every rub, how will the mirror of your heart ever be polished? (Rumi)

Keep your gaze on the bandaged place. That's where the light enters you. (Rumi)

Don't run toward pain and suffering. Just don't run away from them. (Traditional Sufi saying)

Greet the dark thought, the shame, and the malice laughingly. Each has been sent as a guide from beyond. (Rumi)

 # PRACTICE

Do you have a special way of dealing with your difficult feelings? What do you do?

When uncomfortable feelings arise, take time to acknowledge them. Try to become aware of where you experience emotional discomfort in your body. All painful feelings have a corresponding physical sensation located in the body. Find where the physical sensation is located. Then, with mercy and compassion for yourself, simply be present with the feeling as you breathe in and out through that place. Allow divine breath to caress you there. This is an ancient practice called "sacred holding" that will, over time, create healing and integration of the feeling.

Not All Tears Are Equal

"It is He who has created for you hearing, sight, feeling, and understanding," says the Qur'an (23:78; 32:9), from which Sufi teachers conclude that our feelings are from God and are therefore sacred, whether joyous or sorrowful. Happy feelings are easy to accept as gifts, but what about difficult ones, such as suffering or rage? Teachers from many traditions say that these feelings are simply energies begging to be acknowledged, healed, and integrated. We become more developed as humans when we embrace not only our joys but also our sorrows. If we avoid the latter, we do so at our peril. One day those shunned feelings will rise and revolt. Thus, it is essential to embrace, little by little and with compassion for self, the sharp-edged feelings we tend to deny or circumvent.

There are gifts and teachings in moments of pain and suffering, but we can realize these divine favors only when we embrace and integrate the unhappy feelings that they evoke. If we are willing to do that hard spiritual work, we will experience an inner spaciousness and a sense of freedom because, as Rumi says, "Something opens and lifts my wings."

The tears we weep in our difficult moments are the subject of poetic metaphor in Sufi literature. Wherever water flows, life flourishes. Thus our tears are sacred, watering rose gardens in the invisible realms and attracting divine mercy. "Weep like the waterwheel," says Rumi, "so that sweet herbs may grow in the courtyard of your soul."

The Mulla fully agrees, but cautions us that that not all tears are equal. At the funeral of a wealthy man, the Mulla was weeping copiously. Someone asked him if he was a close relative or friend of the deceased. He replied, "I am neither," and added, "and that is why I am crying!"

In another story, the Mulla was crying at a gravesite and saying again and again, "Why did you have to leave so soon?" Touched by this outpouring, a small crowd joined the Mulla and with tears in their eyes asked if the deceased was his child. "Oh no, God forbid!" replied the Mulla. "This is the gravesite of the husband of my wife. I married his widow."

The Mulla is also teaching us that tears lose their sacredness when we get attached to them. While it is absolutely paramount to acknowledge our pain and suffering and do the work of healing and integration, it is also critical not to be devoted to our tears because they have secondary benefits. At a certain point we have to let go. Don't be sad any longer, pleads Rumi, "for your sadness is blasphemy against the Hand of Splendor pouring you joy." In another utterance, he teaches us that in prolonged periods of grief, we need to say to ourselves at the right time, "Enough is enough!" and that "it is time now to speak of roses and pomegranates and of the oceans where pearls are made of language and vision ..."

Just as it is sacred to spend time with our suffering, it is equally sacred to spend time with our blessings. Don't neglect moments of joy in your life. Consciously acknowledge and celebrate them. Feel gratitude for them. Sufi teachers exhort us to do practices where we honor the happy moments in our life and the blessings that come our way.

REFLECTIONS

Continually declare the blessings of your Sustainer! (Qur'an: 93:11)

The bough is made green and fresh by the weeping cloud; the candle is made brighter by its weeping. (Rumi)

For one moment let go of your sadness. Hear blessings dropping their blossoms around you. (Rumi)

PRACTICE

Remember that it is a sacred spiritual practice to celebrate good moments and blessings in your life by humbly and enthusiastically expressing gratitude to your Sustainer.

As a daily practice, recall a time when you felt a life-giving feeling of happiness, joy, passion, or beauty. If this is difficult, use your imagination to conjure up a situation that gives you an assuredly positive feeling. The subconscious does not differentiate between real and imagined. Locate that feeling in your body and with gratitude linger on those moments for as long as you can. Practice this technique daily and you will experience what mystics describe as a spring wind turning the ground green.

Little by Little

Just as the wondrous creation of a child takes nine months and the child requires many years to reach adulthood, it takes a lifetime to evolve into the fullness of our being. Everything happens in its appointed time, says the Qur'an, and it's no use being aggressive or impatient in our pursuit of full spiritual maturity. "So I call to witness the rosy glow of sunset; the night and its progression; and the Moon as it grows into fullness; surely you shall travel from stage to stage" (Qur'an 84:16–19). The Holy Book itself was revealed over a period of time, in "slow well-arranged stages," so that "We may strengthen thy heart" (Qur'an 25:32). Thus the phrase *little by little* is a favorite Sufi mantra to describe the pace of our spiritual growth. An ordinary stick breaks into bud slowly, says Rumi; an ordinary stone marbles into a ruby only in stages.

Whether our work involves inner practices of, say, overcoming fear or outer work of imparting teachings, it is wise to invoke the "little-by-little" mantra as illustrated by a traditional Sufi story called "The Watermelon Hunters." In a strange country called the Land of Fools, a traveling teacher saw people fleeing in terror from their wheat fields. "There's a monster there!" they shouted, but when the teacher went to investigate, he discovered that the "monster" was merely a watermelon. He offered to "kill" the monster, and after he cut it from the stalk he sliced it and even ate a piece to demonstrate that it was harmless. But this only terrified the people even more. "He will end up killing us unless we get rid of him," they cried, and they drove the teacher away with pitchforks. Some time later another teacher ventured into the same land and witnessed the same fear. Aware of the people's primitive consciousness, he acknowledged and appreciated their fear and consequently gained their confidence. He spent a long time with them, earning their trust and teaching them little by little about the real nature of watermelons. Thus the people gradually lost their fear of watermelons and learned to cultivate them for their own enjoyment.

The problem with the little-by-little approach is that we humans are impatient with the incremental grind. We want our progress in quantum leaps, and we want it *now!* We are like the Mulla, who was enamored of Indian classical music and inquired about the cost of enrolling in classes. "Three pieces of silver for the first month, and one piece of silver from the second month onwards," said the master musician. "Great!" replied the Mulla, "Sign me up from the second month!"

The truth is that incremental progress is rewarded from time to time with a quantum leap. "After the difficulty is the easing," says the Qur'an, "so when you are finished, strive again and in your Lord aspire" (94:5–8). Truly, it pays to persist, little by little! But keep in mind, chasms cannot be crossed in small leaps, so be prepared to take large jumps when the situation calls for more direct action.

Leave it to the Mulla to allude to this insight. A cousin was transferred to a distant place and asked the Mulla to keep watch on his favorite donkey and his aging parents. After a few months, the donkey died unexpectedly, and the Mulla sent a message that the donkey was dead. The grieving cousin wrote back, berating the Mulla for not taking a more compassionate approach. He should have softened the blow by breaking the news little by little, said the cousin. He could have started by saying that the donkey was acting a little strange, later that the donkey was refusing food, and then that it was getting weaker and weaker. Finally, the Mulla would be well positioned to break the news that the donkey was dead. The Mulla apologized for his thoughtlessness and promised to mend his ways. After a few months, he sent his cousin a new letter saying, "Your mother is acting a little strange."

REFLECTIONS

Why is the Qur'an not revealed to him all at once? It is so that by this We may strengthen your heart; and We have related it to you in well-arranged stages, little by little." (Qur'an 25:32)

Little by little, wean yourself. This is the gist of what I have to say. From an embryo, whose nourishment comes through the blood, move to an infant drinking milk, to a child on solid food, to a searcher after wisdom, to a hunter of more invisible game. (Rumi)

PRACTICE

Think about times in your life when the little-by-little approach led to a quantum-leap improvement, and draw encouragement from those examples when you feel tempted to give up the daily grind toward spiritual growth.

Name any areas of your life where you need to take more radical action. What might that action be, and how can you accomplish it?

Blessed Are the Flexible

Sometimes it is wise to temper our actions and words with suppleness and elasticity, even going against conventional norms, as long as we can do so without compromising ourselves or our beliefs. In the words of a beloved spiritual principle, "Blessed are the flexible for they will never be bent out of shape!"

The Prophet Muhammad's behavior during prayer times is a beautiful example of this kind of flexibility. The body prayers of standing, bowing, and prostrating in the presence of God are a solemn matter, but the Prophet performed them lightheartedly when he took his granddaughter to the mosque. He would playfully put the child on his shoulder while standing in sacred prayer, set her down beside him during moments of bowing and prostration, and then joyfully pick her up again when standing. He would also shorten the prayers if he heard a child crying for its mother. "I stand in prayer and wish to prolong it," he said. "However, I hear the cry of a child and cut the prayer short for the anxiety that the mother is feeling."[1]

The Mulla also was willing to break conventional rules, this time for practical reasons. A thief followed him into the mosque, and knowing that the man specialized in stealing shoes, the Mulla decided to ignore convention and pray with his shoes on. But the thief could not prevent himself from hissing, "What you are doing is profane. An Islamic prayer said with shoes on does not abide." "Maybe so," whispered the Mulla, "but if the shoes abide, that is at least something!"

Religious rituals are important and, generally speaking, we should perform them if we wish to receive their spiritual benefits. But it is wise not to be so attached to a ritual that we cannot modify it if, despite our best efforts, it is not producing the desired result. An elderly Bedouin once told Muhammad that the rituals of Islam were too complicated for him and asked if the Prophet could recommend just one simple ritual for him to practice. Without a moment's hesitation, the Prophet replied gently, "Keep your tongue forever moistened with the name of Allah."

Flexibility for the sake of compassion can be as sacred as any spiritual practice. God's nature is compassion, says the Qur'an, and occasionally we may be called on to express this divine attribute by suspending or delaying a religious practice in order to accommodate the reasonable desires of someone we love. There was a holy woman who passed her time by praying, fasting and joyously serving everyone she met. The light of purity shone in her and the angels begged God to commemorate her. God created first one star and then another to shine in the skies in her honor. One day when the woman was fasting and praying during the holy month of Ramadan, her little niece visited her and asked her to go for a walk in the forest. On the walk the little girl felt thirsty and hungry but refused to eat and drink unless her aunt joined her. "But I am fasting," said the aunt. "Then, please break your fast," pleaded the little girl. "But God might be angry with me," explained the aunt. "Let God be angry. I just want us to eat and drink together," said the child. With great trepidation, but touched by the little girl's love and not wishing to hurt her feelings, the holy woman broke her fast. And, lo! A third star appeared in her honor!

REFLECTION

The example of a believer is that of a fresh tender plant; from whatever direction the wind comes, it bends with it, but when the wind quiets down, the plant becomes straight again. (*Hadith*)

PRACTICE

Make a conscious effort to become aware of areas in your life where you are rigid and unbending. What makes you realize that you are stern in those places? In what ways can you be more flexible without compromising your values?

A Sense of Balance

The Mulla was apprenticed to a teacher who complained that he wasted time and energy repeating tasks that he should have been able to consolidate more efficiently. For example, rather than going to the market three times to buy one egg each time, the smarter approach would be to go to the market only once and buy three eggs. The Mulla took the lesson to heart. When his teacher became ill and dispatched the Mulla to fetch a doctor, the Mulla returned with four people: two doctors for the sake of a second opinion, an imam who would offer fervent prayers in case the medical treatment did not work, and an undertaker in case nothing worked and the teacher died!

What the Mulla really needed was a lesson not in efficiency but in balance and proportion. We humans often tend to overdo it, whether in thoughts, feelings, words, or deeds. We don't know when to stop, and end up drawing legs on a snake, to quote a Zen metaphor. The Qur'an advises us to pay attention to the divine sense of proportion in the universe. "In true proportions God created the Heavens and the Earth," says a typical verse. "Truly, in that is a sign for those who have faith" (29:44).

We display our lack of balance in many ways, and the Qur'an offers appropriate corrective advice. For example, we easily become attached to our joys and sometimes even to our sorrows, so that we don't make room in our hearts for opposing emotions, but the Qur'an tells us that both laughter and tears are sacred and each should be experienced with equanimity. "Don't despair over things that pass you by nor exult over blessings that come to you" (Qur'an 57:23). If we insist on laughing all the time, even in times of pain and suffering, we miss out on the holiness of tears that water our inner growth. Similarly, if we are overly attached to our tears and regrets, we are, in the words of the poet Tagore, like someone who cries all night long for the daylight and misses out on the beauty of the stars. And if we persist in tasting the bitterness of life in the hope of one day tasting the sweet, we are like the Mulla, who bought some exotic-looking fruits and couldn't stop eating them, even though his tongue felt a painful sting and his eyes began to water. A passerby told him that the fruits were hot chilies native to India and he should stop eating them immediately if he didn't wish to suffer. The Mulla replied that he was actually eating his spent money, and surely at least one of those peppers might turn out to be sweet!

The Qur'an also has advice about concentrating on our spiritual work to the exclusion of the ordinary pleasures of life. "Do not deprive yourself of the good things of life which God has made lawful to you," says the Holy Book, though the same passage also warns us not to transgress "the bounds of what is right" (5:87–88). When we overdo our spiritual practices, we neglect other legitimate claims on our time and energy and are in danger of becoming sanctimonious rather than holy. The Prophet Muhammad counseled his companions not to overdo their spiritual exercises. In their ardent dedication, some of them were fasting all day and praying all night, and the Prophet famously advised them, "Your body has a right over you, your soul has a right over you, and your family and wife have a right over you. So give everyone the right it has over you."

It is hard to tell who was more sanctimonious, the yogi or the Mulla, in the story about the Mulla's fascination with a yogi who publicly declared that he had dedicated his life to the service of all living things, especially birds and fish. "Oh I love fish!" exclaimed the Mulla. "In fact, a big fish once saved my life!" "How extraordinary!" exclaimed the yogi. "This amply substantiates my doctrine that all of God's kingdom is interlinked and we are one indivisible community." The yogi entreated the Mulla to join him in meditation, teachings, and curious gymnastics for several weeks, after which, in a state of purity, they would hold a public discussion of the Mulla's astonishing experience. At the public event, the yogi told the Mulla, "I would be deeply honored if you would kindly communicate your supreme experience with the lifesaving fish. I know that your story will awaken our hearts and minds to the truth of oneness." The Mulla demurred, saying that since he was now more aware of the yogi's piety and philosophy, he was unsure that his story would be relevant. But the yogi begged him with tears in his eyes, calling him "Master" and prostrating himself before the Mulla. "Very well, if you insist," said the Mulla. "At one time in my life I was starving to death. By luck, I was able to net a large fish. The creature from the sea saved my life. It provided me with food for three days!"

REFLECTIONS

Verily, all things have We created in proportion and measure. (Qur'an 54:49)

Always adopt a middle, moderate, regular course whereby you will reach your target of Paradise. (*Hadith*)

A student once told the Mulla that, thanks to him, he had learned to reflect not once but three times before making an important decision and plunging into action. "Once is enough!" said the Mulla.

PRACTICE

In what areas of your life are you feeling unbalanced or overstepping bounds? Make a list and with compassion for self, reflect on them. What are some small changes you could make immediately?

If you are engaging in obsessive thoughts or feelings, do some self-talk whenever you become aware of it. Tell yourself with mercy but firmness, "Stop! I choose to stop. Cancel. Delete." Select words that work for you. Then, take that thought or feeling, place it in your heart, and say, "I release you to Spirit."

If you have a loving and trustworthy circle of friends, or a partner you can be vulnerable with, ask frankly if you tend to exaggerate, are overly critical in your opinions and judgments, or are overstepping limits in any way. If possible, ask them for helpful suggestions. You might be surprised how healing and creative the counsel can be from caring friends and family members.

Web of Interconnection

When you really think about it, our lives are like complex and mysterious webs woven of all the choices we have made, the accidents (both happy and tragic) we have experienced, and the people we have liked or disliked. We may not realize it at the time, but the events and people in our lives are agents of God, who is truly present wherever we may turn. Just take a few minutes right now to review some of the twists and turns that have brought you to this very moment, holding this book in your hands. Are you not astonished by the divine nexus of interconnections in your life?!

The Mulla came to recognize that mysterious web of connection during a dramatic encounter in a graveyard. He had been walking along a deserted road one night when he saw some horsemen racing toward him. His imagination leapt into action and conjured up a terrible fate: He would be captured and sold into slavery or forced into the army. So the Mulla ran for his life, climbed over a wall into a cemetery, and hid in an open grave. Puzzled at his strange behavior, the horsemen—who were honest travelers—followed him and found him stretched out on the ground, quivering with fear. "What's wrong? Why were you running away? What are you doing here?" The Mulla, realizing that his fears had been unfounded, replied in a solemn tone, "The truth, as always, is much more complicated than you might think. You see, I am here in this graveyard because of you, and you are here because of me!"

Sufi teachers remind us that we cannot possibly predict the outcome or meaning of the interweaving of events and people. The multiple factors are beyond human comprehension. A famous story, titled "Bread and Jewels," illustrates this point.

A king who was of a mystical bent decided to give away some precious jewels in a special way. He summoned a baker he trusted and asked him to bake two loaves, one containing the jewels and the other an ordinary loaf made of flour and water. The baker was instructed to give the loaves to the most and least pious persons in the realm.

The following morning, two men presented themselves. One was wearing the robes of a dervish and seemed pious, though in reality he was a charlatan. The other man by coincidence of facial resemblance reminded the baker of someone he distrusted. The baker immediately gave the jewel-encrusted bread to the dervish and the plain bread to the untrustworthy-looking person. The dervish felt the weight of the bread and concluded that there were lumps of unblended flour in it. Realizing that the baker was not a person to trifle with, he decided to fob off the lumpy bread on the other man. "Why not exchange your loaf for mine?" he said. "You look hungry, and this one is larger." The man thought the dervish was being kind, and took the heavier bread with gratitude. The king, who was watching from a hidden place, drew his own conclusions. God must have graced the dervish with divine protection to keep him safe from the dangers of riches. But it was too bad that the other man ended up with the enriched bread, for he appeared quite ordinary and the king imagined he would probably waste the wealth in gambling and drink. In reality, the ordinary-looking man was the most pious person in the realm and spent the wealth in service to others. So who was the true agent of fate in this story? "I did what I was told to do," said the baker. "You cannot tamper with fate," said the king. "How clever I was!" said the false dervish.

REFLECTION

Wherever you turn, there is the Face of Allah. (Qur'an 2:115)

PRACTICE

Which people have had a major impact on your life and what are the watershed events in your life? Write them down in your journal and heighten your awareness of your life journey.

At the end of each day, reflect on the people, incidents, words, sights, and feelings that caught your attention and resonated in you. Express gratitude, extract lessons, and take right action. This regular practice will expand your awareness that the Divine is constantly present in your life in the mysterious guise of myriad people and events.

Thank God for Diversity

"Dear wife!" said the Mulla. "I have figured out a perfect way to play the violin!" Family and friends were duly summoned for an evening of beautiful music, and they listened expectantly as the Mulla, with great fanfare, lifted the instrument to his chin and began to play. Out came a single note, pleasing but not particularly musical. The Mulla drew the bow across the strings again, and out came the same note. Again and again he played the same note, and people began to fidget with discomfort and embarrassment. Finally, his wife asked why he didn't move his fingers on the different strings, as other musicians do. "Well," replied the Mulla, "those other musicians are all struggling to find the perfect note, but I have found it!"

Think what a boring world it would be if the Creator had settled on the "perfect singular note" for creation! Every tree would look alike, every fish and every bird, every human would be a clone of that first man. Thank God for the splendor and diversity of all the things on this Earth, "which He has multiplied in varying hues and qualities" (Qur'an 16:13)! Such mind-boggling variety is a sign of God, says the Qur'an, including "the variations in your languages and your colors: verily in that are signs for those who know" (30:22).

Among those signs is the lesson that variety truly is the spice of life. The Mulla's perfect note was boring and bereft of beauty because he played it repeatedly without variation and did not permit it to harmonize and resonate with other notes. Even compositions of many notes would become tiresome if all we ever heard was the same kind of music over and over again, be it Bach, Beatles, or Bollywood. The same goes for every kind of human culture, whether it be creative arts, religion, or even food. Let's focus on food for a moment, since there is wisdom in the saying, "You are what you eat."

We Americans thrive on a delicious diversity of food, and most of us can't imagine how bored our palates would be without the occasional hint of Thai, Chinese, Indian, Ethiopian, Middle Eastern, Italian, or Mexican flavors, to name just a few that are available almost everywhere in our melting-pot country. But it wasn't always like that. Americans were once extraordinarily resistant to any kind of "ethnic" food and even made a moral issue out of it. In an eye-opening *New York Times* article titled "Immigrant Identities, Preserved in Vinegar?",[2] Jane Ziegelman writes that one of the biggest battles over assimilation occurred a century ago in New York City, and the battleground was food. Politicians, public health experts, and social reformers were alarmed by what they saw as immigrants' excessive use of seasoning in their cooking. They used too much garlic, onion, and pepper and were too generous with the condiments. The officials believed that strongly flavored food caused people to be nervous and unstable, definitely not the best kind of citizen. Amazingly, even the pickle was morally suspect. "As part of a larger effort to Americanize the immigrant kitchen," Ziegelman writes, "culinary crusaders established cooking classes in settlement houses so homemakers could learn to make pies and chowders. They issued bilingual cookbooks that sang the praises of simple American cooking."

This vignette of culinary intolerance shows how difficult it is for us humans to embrace and celebrate the unfamiliar. And if we are so resistant about something as simple and unthreatening as food, it's no surprise that we grapple with bigger issues such as skin color and religion. Even prophets sometimes struggle to open their hearts to those who follow a different path. The twelfth-century sage Al-Ghazzali relates a story about Prophet Abraham, who is highly revered in the Qur'an as the father of monotheism. Abraham made it a spiritual practice to share breakfast with a stranger every morning, and one morning his guest happened to be a fire-worshipping Zoroastrian. When he heard the Zoroastrian invoke the divinity of fire in his prayers, Abraham was incensed and asked the man to leave. Immediately a divine voice proclaimed, "I have fed him for seventy years, but you could not feed him for one time. Had you fed him for just one morning, you would not have become poor on that account."[3] Truly, if we can find the inner spaciousness to be hospitable and kind to those who live and believe differently than we do, it will cost us nothing but a little tweak to the ego. We will not become "poor on that account"; rather, we will be enriched by the encounter with yet another example of the beautiful diversity of God's creation.

REFLECTIONS

Out of this do We bring forth close-growing grain; and out of the spathe of the palm tree, dates in thick clusters; and gardens of vine, and the olive tree, and the pomegranate; all so alike, and yet so different.... verily, in all this there are messages for people who will believe. (Qur'an 6:99)

O God, You have created this I, you, we, they ... to play the game of adoration with Yourself. (Rumi)

 # PRACTICE

Think of a time you had to experience something unknown or unfamiliar. What feelings arose in you, and how did you deal with them? How would you deal with them now?

Sufi teachers ask us not to deny or downplay difficult feelings. When they surface in us, they are begging to be acknowledged, healed, and integrated. If encounters with people who look, live, or believe differently from you cause you to feel uncomfortable, use the technique of sacred holding from the chapter called "Seeking in the Right Direction" to honor your feelings. Then work to heal them, so that you may fully celebrate the many ways in which God is manifested in this wild and wonderful world.

Cultivating Hope through Patience and Faith

An Arab proverb says that a person who has hope has everything. Destroy a person's hope, and you have taken away his or her life. The critical importance of hope is illustrated by a story about the Mulla, who noticed the ticket conductor approaching his compartment on a crowded train. Hurriedly, he began to look for his ticket in other people's pockets and bags. The puzzled and angry passengers asked why he did not search his own pockets and bags. "Indeed, I could do that," the Mulla replied, "But if I do not find the ticket there, I shall lose all hope!"

Hope is not mere expectation or wishful wanting. True abiding hope requires effort, patience, and faith. Twice the Prophet received revelations urging him to be patient despite feeling abandoned and overwhelmed. The first time occurred after the flow of divine messages ceased abruptly and did not resume for three long years. In deep despair, the Prophet intensified his prayers and spiritual practices. Then suddenly, a revelation burst forth:

> By the glorious morning light and by the night when it is still, your Sustainer has not forgotten you, nor is He displeased. And, truly, that which comes after will be better for you than the present. And soon your Sustainer will give that with which you will be content. Didn't He find you an orphan and shelter you? Didn't he find you wandering and guide you? Didn't he find you in need, and satisfy your need? So do not be harsh with orphans, nor turn away one who asks something of you, but continually declare the blessings of your Sustainer! (93:1–11)

The second revelation urging attention to patience and faith came when the Prophet was feeling overwhelmed by unrelenting criticism and attacks from his enemies in Mecca.

If you find their aversion hard to bear, seek if you can a chasm in the Earth or a ladder to the sky by which you may bring them a sign. Had God pleased, He would have given them guidance, one and all. So don't be among those who are swayed by ignorance and impatience. (Qur'an 6:35)

The insights to be gleaned from these two revelations are many. During times of despair, humbly count your blessings; continue with spiritual practices and righteous deeds; and, mostly, be patient and have faith. Eventually, in God's good time and merciful way, your hope will be rewarded. The Qur'an says: He is the One who sends down rain after they have lost all hope and unfolds His Grace (Qur'an 42:28).

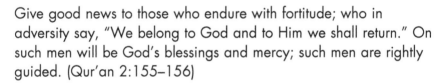

REFLECTIONS

Give good news to those who endure with fortitude; who in adversity say, "We belong to God and to Him we shall return." On such men will be God's blessings and mercy; such men are rightly guided. (Qur'an 2:155–156)

So truly, with every difficulty comes ease: truly with every difficulty comes ease. So when you are free from your task, continue to strive, and to your Sustainer turn with loving attention. (Qur'an 94:5–8)

Whoever submits his or her whole self to God and is a doer of good has indeed grasped the most trustworthy handhold; for with God rests the final outcome of all endeavors. (Qur'an 31:22)

> *Never lose hope, my heart.*
> *Miracles dwell in the Invisible.*
> *If the whole world turns against you*
> *Keep your eyes on the Friend.* (Rumi)

PRACTICE

Think of a time you lost hope and felt forlorn. What helpful actions did you take during that time that eventually restored your sense of peace?

In times of despair, do the following practice: Close your eyes and put your hand on your heart. Feel the beat of your heart. Know that

Divinity resides in that space. Talk silently to your heart. You might say, "Dear Heart, please help me. I surrender to you. Thank you. I love you." Plant words of your choice several times in the magical space of the heart.

The True Teacher
Kindles the Light

We often marvel at the hidden knowledge of birds as they build their nests and bees as they create a honeycomb, but we humans have been gifted with hidden knowledge surpassing anything we see in nature. So unique is this gift, says the Qur'an, that God ordered the angels to bow to the newly created human beings (2:34; 7:11). In the metaphorical language of Rumi, this knowledge is an inner tablet that is already completed and preserved; it does not turn yellow or stagnate and is beyond the normal conduits of learning. It is a divine fountainhead that moves from the inside to the outside.

The role of a spiritual teacher is to help the student connect with this indescribable inner knowing. In the words of a traditional Sufi saying, "The teacher kindles the light; the oil is already in the lamp." Authentic Sufi teachers are adept at tailoring lessons specifically for the needs of individual students to connect with their own essence. The Mulla emulated the ideal Sufi teacher when he gazed intently at a prospective student and asked if he had ever been in love. "No," replied the surprised young man. "First you must go and allow yourself to fall in love. After that experience, come and see me. If you have not trodden the path of love, you are a bird without wings. How can I teach you how to fly if you don't have wings?"

There are many different styles of teaching, and it behooves aspiring students to observe their prospective teachers with an open mind before choosing the one whose methods may be most attuned to their learning styles. Such was the task of a group of students who were thinking about studying with the Mulla. One wintry morning the Mulla advised a student who was about to sip hot tea that he should blow into the beverage to cool it. But that same morning he advised another student, who was shivering with cold, to blow into his cupped hands to warm them. The observing students felt confused and decided that the Mulla's teachings were contradictory and he was a fraud. They could have learned from a South Asian metaphor likening life to a narrow ledge flanked by pits on either side. To those who are walking too far to the right, the master shouts, "Go left!" and to those who are in danger of veering and falling on the left side, the teacher shouts, "Go right!"

Sufi spiritual literature is filled with advice about choice of teachers. One salient piece of advice is to avoid teachers who are overly stern, aggressive, and fiery—teachers whom Rumi describes as "All fire and no light; all husk and no kernel." Also, keep away from teachers who make wild promises about quick enlightenment without hard work. These teachers prey on the lazy, baser aspects of our ego, illustrated by the crowds who responded when the Mulla went to the town square and bellowed, "O people! Listen to what I have to offer. Do you want riches without work, attainment without effort, progress without sacrifice, knowledge without difficulties?" Several times the Mulla repeated this message, and each time the crowd swelled in number and shouted repeatedly, "Yes! Yes! Yes!" At last the Mulla cried out, "Wonderful! Excellent! Thank you! I only wanted to confirm those desires. You can rely on me to tell you about the ways to achieve these goals in good time."

This is the same Mulla who led a group of students through a series of advanced spiritual exercises in which they copied his every move. First they stomped on the ground with vigorous shouts of "Hu! Hu!"; then they became very still; finally they made exotic bird calls. "What are you doing?" a friend asked, and the Mulla replied that he had become an advanced sheikh and was helping his students reach enlightenment. "How do you know when they reach enlightenment?" asked the friend. "That's the easy part," replied the Mulla. "Every morning I count heads. The ones who have left have seen through my antics and realized the foolishness of relying on a teacher. They have reached enlightenment!"

In other words, the Mulla would advise, once you have begun to work with a spiritual teacher, be mindful not to become overly dependent on that teacher's guidance. Remember, a true teacher will want you to evolve into the fullness of your own authentic self and not become a clone of the teacher. It is no credit to either you or the teacher if you sit at his or her feet forever rather than learning to connect with your own inner teacher. The mature student, who has done the work of transforming ego and opening the heart, finally understands the words of the Prophet Muhammad, who emphatically advised, "Consult your heart! Consult your heart! Consult your heart!"

The Mulla was obviously aware of the Prophet's sage advice. He taught a secret practice to his advanced students and warned them to guard it carefully, for it had the power to heal and magically transform. One disciple asked, "What will happen if I share this technique with others?" "You will be cursed!" replied the Mulla. "But will others benefit if I give it to them?" asked the same student. "Yes!" the Mulla said. The next day the student was in the marketplace sharing the mantra with those he discerned would benefit, and his fellow students complained bitterly to the Mulla. "He didn't follow your instructions! Shouldn't he be punished?" With a twinkle in his eye, the Mulla replied, "No! Not at all! He has listened to the teacher in his heart. He has become a real human being. Let him be."

The picture of an ideal Sufi teacher is the image of the Mulla sitting backwards on a donkey followed by students on his right and left, forming a circle. The symbolic meanings are many. The donkey symbolizes the ego. A true teacher has tamed the ego and the donkey knows which way to go. Out of genuine love and respect for his students, the teacher turns his face toward them. He believes in nonhierarchical and collaborative learning; he speaks but also listens attentively. By being willing to teach in unconventional ways, he invites creativity and learning outside the box.

 # REFLECTIONS

Whoever travels without a guide needs two hundred years for a two-day journey. (Rumi)

People think that a sheikh should perform miracles and manifest illumination. The requirement in a teacher, however, is only that he should possess all the disciple needs.[4] (Ibn Arabi)

In nature, small ants do not swarm to see elephants in hope of gain. An illustrious master may be of use only to advanced scholars.[5] (Badakshani)

The true teacher knocks down the idol that the student makes of him.
(Rumi)

PRACTICE

Name the teachers in your life who have influenced you favorably.
In your own style, express prayers of gratitude for them.

Do you believe you have within you an inner teacher? In what
ways has this guide manifested in your life, and what can you do
to honor it?

When a question of guidance comes up in your life, listen to
teachers and authorities, but also place the question in your heart
and sincerely ask your heart for guidance. In stillness, become
aware of feelings and insights that arise and pay attention to them.
With practice, you will learn to discern between the voice of your
ego and the voice of your higher self. The Qur'an says that the
heart never falsifies what it sees.

Knowing God

Connecting to Mystery

"Allah is the Light of the Heavens and the Earth," sings the Holy Qur'an in a revelation so mysterious that it has its own name, the "Verse of Light" (24:35). Indeed, God is the ultimate mystery: invisible despite the appellation of light, formless, genderless, eternally enveloping and permeating all of creation. With our limited human faculties, it is futile to attempt to quantify the magnitude and magnificence of God. "And even if all the trees on Earth were pens, and the oceans ink, backed by seven more oceans, the Words of God would not be exhausted," says the Holy Book (31:27).

Even so, we humans insist on defining the undefinable and dividing the indivisible, often fighting and even killing each other over our dogmatic definitions and minuscule understandings of God. Hafiz alludes to this tragic behavior in a tale about a group of thieves who stole a large diamond of inestimable value and celebrated by getting drunk. In their drunkenness they got into a brawl and decided to divide the precious stone into pieces. Of course, the priceless gem was lost in the process. Hafiz concludes, in a delightful translation by Daniel Ladinsky, "Most everyone is lousy at math and does that to God." Each one thinks, "This is my Beloved" and "How could that moron over there really be God?"[1]

Another enigmatic verse in the Qur'an says, "Everywhere you turn is the Face of Allah." A Mulla story provides a partial insight into the many facets of this revelation. The Mulla journeyed to the sacred Kabah in Mecca and after hours of prayer and meditation, he fell asleep in the grand mosque. His feet happened to point in the direction of the sacred Kabah, and this offended some Meccans, who woke him and informed him how disrespectful it was to point his feet in the direction of the House of Allah. "Apologies for my ignorance," said the Mulla. "Please take my feet and place them in the direction where Allah is not." At this, the chastened Meccans left the Mulla alone.

If we truly take this verse to heart and reflect on the Mulla story, we shall see God in the face of every human being, whether friend or foe. We can never harbor hate for anyone or anything. In our relationship with an adversary, for example, our hearts will be able to distinguish between behavior and being. An opponent's behavior may be unacceptable, and we must take right action to protect ourselves and seek justice. However, we must do that with respect for that person's Allah essence that is hidden by layers of personality and life circumstances. Developing the heart's ability to discern between behavior and being has the power to shift Heaven and Earth.

In another mysterious verse God says, "We are closer to you than your jugular vein" (Qur'an 50:16). Echoing that statement of intimate proximity are the astonishing words revealed to the Prophet in a dream, "Neither my Heaven nor my Earth can contain me, but the soft humble heart of my believing slave can contain me." We simply have to open our hearts to the astonishing truth that God is present within us at every moment. The ninth-century Sufi master Salih of Qazwin was telling his students that they must persist in knocking on Divinity's door and out of divine grace and compassion, Allah surely will open the door one day. The sage Rabia was passing by and overheard the teaching. "Brother," she asked, "when was the door ever closed?" In response, Salih rose and bowed his head.

Is God boundlessly compassionate and infinitely merciful as the Qur'an tells us? If so, how is it possible that there is so much pain, suffering, injustice, and cruelty in the world? To such a question there is no human answer that will satisfy us. But what is truly astonishing is that some of the most ardent devotees of God are those who have been at one time savaged by life's circumstances and felt betrayed by God. After a period of healing, their faith and connection to Mystery has deepened substantially. A Bedouin was asked if he had faith in the All-Compassionate God. The Bedouin replied, "You mean the God who has sent me afflictions, poverty, and made me wander from country to country?" But as he spoke, he entered into a state of ecstasy.

In a similar vein that reflects mystery and a deeper truth, Rumi recites a poem in which some people proclaim, "The Beloved is so sweet, so sweet," and Rumi replies, "I show them my scars where His polo stick thrashed me." Now they declare, "The Beloved is terrible! A maniac! A monster!" Rumi then says, "I show them my eyes, melting in His tender passion."

How can we tell if we have been graced by the Light or by what mystics call the Glow of Presence? A villager rushed to the Mulla and exclaimed that for the past week he had been having visions of God, and the Light of Splendor poured upon him. Excitedly, he asked the Mulla if this meant that he was becoming enlightened. Calmly, the Mulla asked, "How many goats do you have?" "I tell you about divine Light and you ask me about goats? What do you mean?" The Mulla continued, "How many servants do you have?" The man became agitated. "Your questions are nonsensical!" The Mulla explained, "If you have become more tender in your caring about your goats and more compassionate in your behavior with your servants, then certainly I would say that your visions are authentic. If not, they are simply an illusion of your ego."

REFLECTIONS

Whoever knows God, his tongue falters. (*Hadith*)

You say you have seen Him, but your eyes are two stones. You say you have known Him, but nothing in you trembles. (Rumi)

I concerned myself to remember God, to know Him, to love Him and to seek Him. When I had come to the end I saw that He had remembered me before I remembered Him, that His knowledge of me had preceded my knowledge of Him, that His love for me had existed before my love for Him and He had sought me before I sought Him.[2] (Bayazid Bistami)

If I say He is within me, the entire Universe hangs its head in shame; yet if I say he is outside of me, I know I am a liar.[3] (Kabir)

PRACTICE

Do you find yourself wanting to connect with God only in times of difficulties? What would be a simple but effective daily practice for you to bond with your Sustainer at all times?

Sit quietly, close your eyes, focus your attention on your nostrils, and simply be mindful of your breath as you inhale and exhale.

With each inbreath and outbreath, silently say, "Allah," or any name for Divinity that feels comfortable to you. With continuous practice you will find yourself bonding with Mystery inside and outside of you.

In a meditative state, focus on your heart and become aware of the astonishing truth that divine Heart resides within human heart. Place your hand on your heart and tell that space where Divinity resides, "I love You" or "Please help me to love You." Choose words that feel right to you, and say them with feeling and sincerity. If this feels awkward, remind yourself that you are directing your words to your Sustainer. Follow up with another set of words about gratitude, "I am so grateful. Thank you." Or "Please open my heart to gratitude." Regular practitioners of this technique report being embraced by a mysterious peace and love.

If God Wills

The skeptics of Mecca sought to discredit the Prophet by commissioning Christian and Jewish scholars to come up with difficult questions that only a prophet could answer. When they presented one such question to Muhammad, he told them the answer would be forthcoming the next day. But there was neither manifestation of angel Gabriel nor a revelation the next day or the day after that. After fifteen long and trying days, finally a revelation burst forth containing a full answer to the question, followed by a cardinal message: "Do not say of anything, 'I shall be sure to do so and so tomorrow' without adding, 'If God wills'" (Qur'an 18:23–24).

This verse has so permeated the Muslim soul that children learn from an early age to say *Inshallah,* meaning "if God wills," whenever they speak about what they are going to do, whether in the next instant or a month from now. *Inshallah* is our implicit acknowledgment that God is the final arbiter of whatever transpires in our lives and we are not completely self-sufficient.

The Qur'an's advice to say *Inshallah* is a beautiful spiritual practice, as long as we do it consciously and do not use it to justify our weaknesses and shortcomings. The Mulla had no patience with that misuse of the phrase. Having saved up enough money to get a new shirt, he went to a tailor's shop full of excitement. The tailor measured him and said, "Come back in a week, and, God willing, your shirt will be ready." The Mulla contained himself for a week and then went back to the shop. "Unfortunately, there has been a delay," said the tailor, "but, God willing, your shirt will be ready tomorrow." The following day the Mulla returned. "I am sorry," said the tailor, "but it is not quite finished. Try tomorrow, and, God willing, it will be ready." By now thoroughly fed up, the Mulla exclaimed, "How long will it take if you leave God out of it?!"

The danger of overusing *Inshallah* is illustrated in a fascinating article in the *New York Times.* Writing about the routine use of *Inshallah* in Cairo, the author, Michael Slackman, says there has been

"*Inshallah* creep to the extreme," calling it "a reflex, a bit of a linguistic tic that has attached itself to nearly every moment, every question, like the word 'like' in English." He goes on to remark that the word has become a convenience and a dodge to avoid commitment. No need to say no. If it doesn't happen, "Well, God didn't mean it to happen." Some people use the word so mindlessly, Slackman says, that even a question about someone's name might be answered, "Muhammad, *Inshallah*."[4]

The overuse of *Inshallah* or any sacred word makes it meaningless and the Mulla pokes ample fun at those who do it. But he also seems to suggest that it is equally foolhardy to be defiantly opposed to using any sacred words whatsoever.

One evening the Mulla announced to his wife that if the weather were sunny the next day, he would plow the field. If it rained, he would gather firewood from the forest. "Say *Inshallah*," his wife told him. "That's stupid and ridiculous," replied the Mulla, "Either it will rain or not rain, and I have decided what to do in either case." The Sun was out the next day and the Mulla set out to plow his field. On the way, he met some soldiers who asked him the way to the next village. Not wishing to waste time, he replied in an unhelpful tone that he had absolutely no idea. Offended by the Mulla's attitude, they started beating him and saying, "Maybe this will help you remember." "I remember now," shouted the Mulla. The soldiers forced him to lead the way. On the way it started to rain and by the time he arrived at the village he was drenched and sore. When he returned home past midnight, he was exhausted and humbled. He knocked on the door. "Who is it?" called out his wife. The Mulla replied, "It is I, *Inshallah!*"

 REFLECTIONS

Truly the knowledge of the Last Hour is with God alone. It is He who sends down rain and He who knows what is within the wombs. Nor does anyone know what it is that he will earn the coming day; nor does anyone know in what land he is to die. Truly, with God is complete knowledge and He is All-Aware. (Qur'an 31:34)

If one desires the rewards of this world, let him remember that with God are the rewards of both this world and the life to come. (Qur'an 4:134)

And make not Allah's name an excuse in your oaths against doing good, or acting rightly, or making peace between persons; for Allah is One who hears and knows all things. (Qur'an 2:224)

 # PRACTICE

What has been your experience in your family hearing the name of God invoked? Did it have positive or negative connotations?

Do you believe it is good or necessary to invoke the name of Divinity in your everyday conversations? How often do you actually do it?

If the mention of God is not part of your daily conversation, try it for a few days and see how it feels. Use a name for Divinity that feels right to you, for example, Holy One, Beloved, Creator, Spirit. If it makes you uncomfortable or feels artificial, don't force it—but strive to connect with Divinity silently in your own heart frequently throughout the day.

Be Engaged
in the World

Do What Is Beautiful

According to the Holy Book, each one of us was born to be a representative of God on Earth, entrusted with the care of God's creation (6:165). In various interpretations of the Qur'an (all "translations" are actually interpretations), we are called "viceroys," "vice-regents," or "vicegerents." The first two terms, based on the French *roi* and the Latin *rex,* meaning "king," indicate our role as deputies of God the "King," while "vicegerent," based on the Latin *gerens,* or "conducting," defines that role as carrying on God's business in the world. Small wonder, then, that the Qur'an instructs us to behave in ways that represent the qualities of our divine Deputizer. "Persevere in doing good," says the Holy Book, "for God loves the doers of good" (2:195).

With these thoughts in mind, the Mulla sprang into action one moonlit night when he passed a well and saw to his horror that the Moon had fallen into the well. Eager to be of service, he rushed home and got a rope. Then he rushed back, tied a hook to the rope, and flung it into the well. "Worry not, sister Moon," he crooned. "Help is at hand!" The hook snagged on something in the well, and the Mulla heaved and pulled with all his might. Suddenly the hook came loose and the momentum threw the Mulla onto his back. Looking up at the sky, he was elated to find the Moon restored to its proper domain! "Thank God, I happened to be passing this way," he said to himself. "Who knows what would have happened to the Moon without my help!"

As this story illustrates, intention and sincerity are beautiful qualities, but genuine acts of service also have to be accompanied by higher awareness. The Mulla's actions to save the Moon were funny and harmless, but sometimes our acts of "service," individually and collectively, can injure others. As the Prophet Muhammad once said, "More harm is done by fools through foolishness than is done by evildoers through wickedness." Such was the case when the Mulla made it his life's mission to pluck the fish out of neighborhood ponds to save them from a watery grave. His intentions may have been pure, but his actions were disastrous for the fish!

Rather than worrying about a grand mission, as the Mulla does, it is wiser for us to cultivate an attitude and habit of service in our everyday life. The Qur'an has clear guidelines: Give freely of what you love; give to those who ask and don't ask; and, when possible, do your service in secret, for this will atone for some of your wrongdoings.

One of the most beautiful things we can do, and something that will contribute immeasurably to goodness in this world, is to ensure that our speech is kind and compassionate. The majority of our sins emanate from our tongue, said the Prophet, so "Whoever believes in Allah and the Last Day should say something good or remain silent." Gossip and insults are bad enough, but even worse is our human tendency to embellish on them. The Mulla showed his darker side while gossiping about Abdul with his friends in the teahouse. As criticisms mounted, someone remarked that Abdul was as useless as a cabbage. "That is an unfair comparison," objected the Mulla. "A cabbage can at least be boiled, cooked, and eaten. But of what use is Abdul?" A mindless habit of criticism and gossip has a way of extending disrespectfully even into solemn occasions. Years later, in the same teahouse, it was reported that Abdul had died, and someone asked, "What was the cause?" To which the Mulla chimed in, "No one knows the reason for his being alive, let alone the cause of his death!"

It should be clear from these unkind stories that one of the noblest acts of service is to restrain ourselves from criticizing others. There is a practical benefit as well: "Veil the faults of others so that yours might be veiled," says Rumi, and the Qur'an advises that "Kind words and covering of faults are better than charity followed by injury" (2:263).

Whether in speech or action, our most beautiful deeds are those that are infused with graciousness and generosity. A famous traditional Islamic saying tells us that "The true character of a friend of God is based on nothing more than graciousness and generosity." It will become second nature to be a friend of God—and a vice-regent and vicegerent—if we take to heart these words of the Prophet: "Do good deeds according to your capacity. God does not grow tired of giving rewards unless you tire of doing good. The good deeds most loved by God are those that are done regularly, even if they are small."

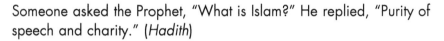 REFLECTIONS

Someone asked the Prophet, "What is Islam?" He replied, "Purity of speech and charity." (*Hadith*)

If kindness were a visible creation, nothing that Allah has created would be more beautiful than it. (*Hadith*)

The Garden is the abode of the Generous. (*Hadith*)

 PRACTICE

Become aware of your choice of words and your tone of voice. Without compromising the content of your speech, how can you be more kind and courteous?

Are you aware of doing any act of service that is actually not helpful to the recipient? If so, what changes can you make?

In what ways can you be more gracious and generous with family, friends, colleagues, strangers, and people who annoy you?

Make a commitment to engage daily in beautiful deeds no matter how small: a smile, a greeting, small courtesies, a helping hand, a quiet prayer, and a blessing for the other.

Remember to make time to nurture and nourish yourself. Take rest, engage in silence, pray, and practice owning your own sorrows with kindness and mercy for yourself. This is not only a service to you, it increases your capacity to help others.

Building Community

We humans are social animals and even the most spiritual among us need community for our physical and spiritual well-being. Drawing from nature, as he often does, Rumi observes that the grapevine needs companionship with the ground in order to grow, and reeds will make a useful mat when woven together but will blow away when left on their own. A wall standing alone will fall to the ground, but when joined with other walls it will support a roof to keep grain safe and dry.

The Qur'an urges us to cultivate a community that will "encourage the doing of what is right and forbid the doing of what is wrong" (3:104) and tells us to conduct our affairs by "mutual consultation" (42:38).

Despite our individual dysfunctions, we can reach our destination of becoming whole if we are willing to collaborate with each other, as illustrated by the classic tale of two men, one lame and the other blind, who were invited to the king's banquet. Both men despaired of going because of their handicaps: the journey was too long and difficult for the lame man, and the blind man would not be able to find his way. But when they lamented their difficulty at a community gathering, the Mulla came up with a creative solution: The lame man could piggyback on the blind man and use his eyes to guide the strong legs of his blind companion. Because of community input and their mutual cooperation, both men were able to attend the king's banquet.

An often-quoted chapter of the Qur'an says that humanity, by virtue of time, is lost and forlorn except for those who have faith and do righteous deeds and who join together in community to support one another to learn about truth and patience (103:1–3). Sufi teachers agree that the best and most effective learning comes not from experts or authorities but from community members who share teachings and experiences with one another at the grassroots level.

The Mulla illustrated this truth when he was invited to preach at the local mosque. "O believers," he asked, "do you know the theme of my talk?" "We have no idea," they replied. Declaring that it was useless to scatter the seeds of his wisdom on the stony ground of their ignorance, the Mulla stepped down from the pulpit and left the mosque. The following week, having been persuaded to return to the pulpit, he asked again, "Do you know what I am going to talk about today?" This time the congregation roared back, "Yes!" but to everyone's surprise, the Mulla stepped down again. "If you already know," he said, "what is the use of my telling you and wasting my time and yours?" Once again the long-suffering mosque officials asked the Mulla to return, and this time the congregation members were prepared. When he asked the expected question, some said yes and some said no. But again the Mulla stepped down, this time saying, "In that case, let those who know teach those who don't know!"

Most of us have several communities or circles in our lives—family, friends, work associates, fellow hobbyists—but the most precious circle we are asked to cultivate is what Rumi calls the "circle of love." This is an intimate circle of people who meet three essential qualifications: mutual love, mutual trust, and mutual regard for truth. These qualifications are highly selective and those who meet them may be few, but the combination of inner work and heartfelt yearning for authentic community will eventually manifest in your own personal circle of love. This will deeply enrich your spiritual life.

REFLECTIONS

Help one another in righteousness and piety. (Qur'an 5:2)

Ordinary people are friendly with those who are outwardly similar to them. The wise are friendly with those who are inwardly similar to them. (Traditional Sufi saying)

With company, you quicken your ascent. You may be happy enough going alone, but with others you get further and further. (Rumi)

Come out of the circle of time and enter the circle of love. (Rumi)

PRACTICE

Who are the people in your life who qualify—through mutual love, trust, and regard for truth—to be in your circle of love? Try to spend time with them—laughing, crying, and sharing the grand adventure of spiritual growth and exploration.

Whenever you meet anyone, focus on your heart and intentionally send light and love to that person's soul or essence. If you meet someone you dislike, remind yourself that you are radiating light and love not to the person's personality but to the person's soul. This is one of the quickest ways for a circle of love to manifest in your life.

Justice and Conflict Resolution

"My Lord has commanded justice," says the Holy Book (7:29), and numerous revelations offer guidelines on how to live with each other justly and harmoniously. A particularly powerful verse tells us to bear witness to the truth in complete fairness, regardless of our personal feelings and animosities, and ends with a command that is dear to the Sufi heart: "Be just: This is the closest to being God-conscious" (5:8).

Practicing justice might seem to be an obvious proposition, but the truth is that issues are not always as clear-cut and easy to discern as we think they should be. We have only to look at a family quarrel from the differing points of view of all the aggrieved parties to realize that a simple computation of rights and wrongs that have accumulated over time will not always help us arrive at a just decision about how to solve the conflict.

The Mulla recognized this problem when he was asked to judge a dispute between two villagers. After hearing the plaintiff's case, he declared, "You are right!" But then, after hearing the defendant's side of the story, he again proclaimed, "You are right!" The bailiff complained, "Your honor, how can both the plaintiff and the defendant be right at the same time?" "You are right!" exclaimed the Mulla.

Sometimes the best way to achieve justice is to facilitate healing through the process of forgiveness and reconciliation. There are many ways of going about this, some of them quite creative. The Prophet, for example, chose not to adjudicate between his daughter and her husband during a marital dispute, but instead to serve as a literal conduit for them to exchange more loving vibrations. Lying down between them, he asked each of them to put a hand on his belly and to breathe with him. After some time spent in that unitive rhythm of breathing, the couple relaxed into a peaceful state and realized that the sharp edges of their dispute had dissolved.[1]

Whenever we are trying to help resolve a conflict, the first step is to realize that the cause may not be what we think it is. The Mulla was awakened by a commotion outside his house and went out to investigate, wrapped only in a blanket. Two men were fighting, but when they saw the Mulla's blanket one of them grabbed it and ran away. When he went back inside, his wife asked what the fight was about. "They were fighting over my blanket," said the Mulla. "As soon as they took it from me, the fight was over!"

Many of us go searching in the leaves and branches, to use Rumi's metaphor, when the cause of a conflict really appears in the roots. And at the root, we will usually find that egos have been bruised and hurt. All the excuses given for the conflict are simply different ways of assuaging an inflamed or wounded ego. The Prophet understood this fundamental truth when a serious dispute arose between various clans about who should place a sacred black stone in the corner of the Kabah. All the clans had worked together to rebuild the Kabah, the symbolic House of God, but when it came to the honor of placing the stone, the clans were ready to battle each other. After hearing the arguments of the clan leaders, the Prophet asked for a robe, maneuvered the stone into the center, and then asked all the clan leaders to grasp different sides of the robe and together raise and position the stone in the Kabah. Thus, instead of trying to choose the "most worthy" clan and alienating the others, the Prophet soothed wounded egos and allowed everyone to enjoy the singular honor of placing the stone together.

There are times when "justice" may seem to demand punishment for a crime, but Sufis prefer to think in terms of "restorative justice." This kind of justice focuses not on punishment but on rehabilitation through dialogue and reconciliation among the offender and the victims or survivors and the community at large. Of course, the financial and emotional needs of victims must be met, but Sufi teachers are skeptical about the value of punishment, either as restitution to the victim or as a deterrent against future crime.

This is well illustrated in the story of the Mulla who asked his son to fetch water from the well in a glass pitcher. "Make sure you don't break the pitcher," the Mulla said, and before handing the pitcher to the child, the Mulla spanked him. The Mulla's wife intervened, exclaiming, "Why did you spank him when he hasn't broken the pitcher?" The Mulla replied, "Of what use would it be if I punish him after he breaks the jug?"

REFLECTIONS

Behold, God enjoins justice, and the doing of good, and generosity toward [one's] fellow people. (Qur'an 16:90)

Repel evil with what is better: then will he between whom and you was hatred become as it were your friend and intimate!
(Qur'an 41:34)

If you are patient in adversity and forgive—this, behold, is indeed something to set your heart upon! (Qur'an 42:43)

If a man gives up quarreling when he is in the wrong, a house will be built for him in Paradise. But if a man gives up a conflict even when he is in the right, a house will be built for him in the loftiest part of Paradise."[2] (*Hadith*)

PRACTICE

Describe an experience when you were asked to take sides in conflicts between family members or friends. How did you handle the situation? What would you do differently today?

What kind of conflicts are you currently experiencing in your life, and what are some creative ways to heal or resolve them?

Revere the Wombs
That Bore You

As a child the Mulla walked to school with his friends along a mountain trail, where they daily encountered a woman who was tending a herd of donkeys. Being mischievous and disrespectful, they taunted her by bowing to her and shouting, "Good morning, mother of donkeys!" The woman smiled patiently, but one day she responded to their impertinent remarks. "Good morning, mother of donkeys!" they called out as usual, and she, without missing a beat, replied, "Good morning, my children!" In Sufi literature, the donkey is a symbol of the undeveloped ego and those children were demonstrating their conditioned bias against women, which they had learned from their unenlightened fathers and uncles in their mountain village. Sadly, city men of the Mulla's culture often are no more enlightened than their country cousins, and for centuries women have had to endure societal prejudices and misogynistic religious customs. Until men do the inconvenient work of transforming their undeveloped egos, no amount of admonition, legislation, or penalties will structurally transform the centuries-old biases that favor men and exclude women from their rightful place in the world.

A true story about the Sufi sage Rabia illustrates the kind of disrespect even the most enlightened women have had to bear. One day a group of men confronted her and boasted, "The crown of prophethood has been placed on men's heads. The belt of nobility has been fastened around men's waists. No woman has ever been a prophet." "Ah," replied Rabia, "but egoism and self-worship and 'I am your Lord most high' have never sprung from a woman's breast. All these have been the specialty of men."

It is important to note that bias against women is most definitely not an Islamic value. It may be endemic in some Muslim cultures, but that is a function of tribal traditions and fabricated misogynistic *hadith,* not religious beliefs. A chapter of the Qur'an titled "The Women" opens with the admonition to "Reverence your Guardian-Lord ... and reverence the wombs that bore you: for Allah ever watches over you" (4:1). This is not the language of a religion that would deny the essential creativity of half the human race.

Indeed, Islamic spiritual teachers point out that the divine principle of creativity is expressed through the feminine, and the two divine traits mentioned most frequently in the Qur'an are mercy and compassion, which are feminine words based on the Arabic root meaning "womb." Based upon Chapter 19 of the Qur'an, titled *Maryam,* or Mary, spiritual teachers ask us to reflect on the truth that the birth of Jesus required the sacred womb of Mary. The teaching here is that until we infuse our beings with divine feminine qualities, we cannot give birth to our inner Jesus or our higher self. The twelfth-century sage Ibn Arabi declared that the most perfect vision of God is enjoyed by those who contemplate Divinity in woman.[3] Rumi uttered, "Woman is a ray of God!"

REFLECTIONS

For men and women who surrender themselves to God ... and for men and women who remember God unceasingly, for them God has readied forgiveness and a supreme recompense. (Qur'an 33:35)

Women are the twin halves of men. (*Hadith*)

It is He who has created you all out of one soul, and out of it brought into being a mate, so that man might incline with love toward woman. (Qur'an 7:189)

The rights of women are sacred. See to it that they are maintained in the rights assigned to them. (*Hadith*)

PRACTICE

What kind of gender bias do you see in yourself, in family members, and in your community? Reflect on the source of these prejudices and think about what you can do to help change attitudes in your personal sphere of influence.

What kind of customs does your religion follow that are unfair to women, and what kind of changes would you like to see? How can you help to make a difference in your place of worship?

Even though God is described as genderless in monotheistic traditions, Divinity always appears in the holy books in the masculine gender. Make a deliberate and conscious effort to refer to God in the feminine gender as often as in the masculine gender.

Advice on Marriage

"Marriage is half of religion," said the Prophet Muhammad, suggesting that half of our growth and learning comes from the lifetime experience of a sacred union with our spouse. The Qur'an declares that husband and wife are "protectors of each other" (9:71) and "garments to each other" (2:187). In their union they experience the mystery of Divinity:

> *Among the Signs of God is this*
> *That God created for you mates*
> *From among yourselves*
> *That you may dwell in tranquility with them,*
> *And God engenders love and compassion between you;*
> *Truly in that are signs for those who reflect.* (30:21)

In addition to the words of the Qur'an, the Mulla has three pieces of advice on marriage. First, we should not be wrapped in our egos searching for the "perfect" mate. The Mulla wasted half his life looking for the perfect wife. After a long search, he met a woman in Damascus who was almost perfect: she was gorgeous, but was of only medium height and he wanted his children to be tall. In Baghdad, he met a woman who was beautiful and tall, but had an unpleasant voice. How could he spend a lifetime listening to a voice like that? In Cairo he finally met the absolutely perfect woman! She was tall, stunning, and had the voice of an angel. When asked why he didn't marry her, the Mulla replied, "Unfortunately, she also was looking for the perfect partner."

The Mulla's second piece of advice concerns the motives of Muslim polygamists who quote the Qur'an to justify taking multiple wives. The Holy Book does permit the practice in theory, although the passage occurs only once and was meant to protect and provide for orphans and widows in the time of war in seventh-century Arabia. Even in those exceptional circumstances, however, the revelation clearly states that multiple marriages are permissible only if the husband is able to divide his affection equally among his wives, which, the Qur'an says, is virtually impossible: "You will never be able to deal equitably with all your wives, however much you want" (4:129).

The well-meaning Mulla proves that point. Every day his two wives asked him which was his favorite, and every day he assured them that he loved them equally. Not satisfied with his answer, the younger and prettier of the two wives posed a practical question: "If we both fell into a river, whom would you save first?" The Mulla turned to his older wife, put his arms around her, and asked, "You know how to swim, don't you, dear?"

The Mulla's third piece of advice is for divorcees, widows, and widowers who remarry. The Mulla counsels this group of potential marriage partners to heal their grief before entering into another marriage. Soon after his wife died, the Mulla married a widow. They talked often about their former spouses, and one night in bed the conversation about their deceased spouses went on and on. Suddenly, the Mulla shoved his wife off the bed. She of course was very upset and complained about the incident to her brother. When the brother confronted him, the Mulla explained that it was not his fault: "The truth is that with my late wife and your sister's deceased husband, there were four of us in the bed. There wasn't room for all of us, and she just fell off the bed!"

 # REFLECTIONS

O humankind! We created you from a single (pair) of male and female ... that you may know each other. (Qur'an 49:13)

Our Lord, let our spouses and children be a source of joy for us. (Qur'an 25:74)

 # PRACTICE

If marriage is a sacred union of body and soul, what steps can we take to get to know our partner beyond personality?

In what ways can we help each other heal our past wounds and fears?

Can we together create a daily ritual that invites Presence or Spirit into the relationship?

Honor the Children

"To God belongs the dominion of the Heavens and the Earth. He creates what He wills. He bestows children male or female according to His Will" (42:49). Thus speaks the Qur'an about the gift of children, suggesting that children are not the exclusive right or privilege of their parents but should be treasured as a gift and reared in a way that honors their Creator.

Sufi teachers have some useful advice about children, starting with the need to be realistic about children's abilities and talents. This is particularly important in our current age, when children are pushed relentlessly to excel on the one hand and rewarded disproportionately for the slightest accomplishments on the other hand. It may seem natural to believe that one's own children are the brightest and best of the lot, but take a lesson from the Mulla, who was deluded by a similar bias. The Mulla's son was chattering away one day and suddenly declared, "Father, I can remember the day you were born!" Looking proudly at his wife, the Mulla exclaimed, "Our son is a genius!"

Just as we need to be honest in our appraisals of our beautiful children, we also need to speak truthfully to them and honor their instinct for the truth. Be wary of little white lies. If we use them to appease our children or silence their curiosity, that strategy may backfire. The Mulla's son was at the age when he was asking questions constantly, and the Mulla was at wit's end. Finally the child asked one more question: "Father, why do you have some white hair?" "Because," the Mulla snapped, "when children keep on asking impossible questions, they make a father's hair grow white." "Oh," replied the son. "That explains why grandfather's hair is white as snow!"

As in our speech, also in our actions we must model the way we wish our children to behave. Children are natural mimics, and quickly learn to behave as their parents do. For example, if they see their parents manipulating each other or feel manipulated themselves, they will promptly learn the tricks of the trade. The Mulla's son thought he could con his father by telling him excitedly, "I had a wonderful dream last night. An angel whispered some future good news into your right ear. You were so happy that you gave me a five-rupee note." But the Mulla was too quick to fall for the con. "That is truly wonderful," he said. "And since you have been such a good boy, I'll let you keep it!"

The day-to-day grind of rearing a child is difficult and, at times, exasperating. But children are also a source of deep happiness and fulfillment. They can impart amazing insights that make the sacred task a joy and a blessing. Such an insight occurred when the eighth-century teacher Hasan of Basra pointed to the flame of a candle and asked a child, "Tell me, little one, where did this magical flame come from?" The child looked at the teacher and then at the flame and suddenly blew out the flame. "You tell me," the child asked, "where did the flame go?" Hasan of Basra later remarked that this little child taught him an important lesson about the mystery of life.

The most important spiritual teaching about children is that they are a gift from the Creator and each one should be welcomed and valued, male and female alike. It is astonishing how discriminatory religious customs and tribal cultures can hold us in their grip. At a time in the seventh century when the Prophet lost his only surviving son in infancy and the opposing tribes taunted him for having no male heir, he turned to God in lamentation and sorrow. Immediately, a revelation burst forth: "To thee We have granted the fount [of Abundance]. Therefore to thy Lord turn in prayer and sacrifice" (Qur'an 108:1–2). This is a remarkable verse. The divine message is that the fullness of life comes not from fulfilling tribal patrilineal expectations but from being conscious of God and being of service to God's creation.

REFLECTIONS

Every child comes with the message that God is not yet discouraged of man.[4] (Tagore)

And so, when he has embraced her, she conceives a light burden, and continues to bear it. Then, when she grows heavy, they both pray to God, their Sustainer: "If You grant us a righteous child, we shall most certainly be among the grateful." (Qur'an 7:189)

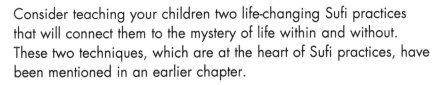

PRACTICE

Consider teaching your children two life-changing Sufi practices that will connect them to the mystery of life within and without. These two techniques, which are at the heart of Sufi practices, have been mentioned in an earlier chapter.

> Touch your heart and tell the space of your heart,
> "I love you" and "I thank you."

> Focus on your heart and send out light and love to the essence of everything you see.

These practices might initially feel awkward to adults, but children will adopt them readily and enjoy the sense of connectedness they impart.

Time to
Return Home

It's Later Than You Think

"Time flies when you're having fun," the saying goes—especially when you're visiting the London Museum with the Mulla. After hearing a tour guide announce that a certain artifact was five thousand years old, the Mulla stepped forward importantly and declared, "Actually, it's five thousand and four years old." The tour members were impressed with his knowledge, but the guide sniffed with annoyance. A few minutes later the guide pointed to a vase and said it was ten thousand years old. The tour group murmured in awe, but again the Mulla interrupted to declare that the vase was actually ten thousand and four years old. "Sir," said the indignant guide, "I assume from your turban that you are from the inscrutable East and possess a mysterious knowledge, but how can you be so precise about the dates?" "Oh, that's simple," replied the Mulla. "I heard you announce those very same dates when I was here four years ago."

Indeed, it's later than the tour guide thought, and it would be prudent for him—and all of us—to consider the spiritual consequences of the rapid passage of time. Did we use our time wisely to fulfill our goals and aspirations? Did we work to transform our egos? Did we take time to serve God's creation? Did we fulfill God's purpose for us on Earth? The fifteenth-century mystic Kabir does not mince words. If you do not break your ropes here on Earth, he asks, do you think ghosts are going to do it for you on the other side? The Qur'an asks directly, "Has not the time arrived for the believers that their hearts in all humility should engage in the remembrance of Allah and of the Truth which has been revealed to them?" (Qur'an 57:16).

One of the great mysteries of time is that cause and effect are not linear. What you will be doing next week may well not be the effect but the cause of what is happening to you today. The Mulla taught that lesson to the attendants at the local bathhouse. One day he went in dressed as a peasant, and the attendants paid him scant attention. Nevertheless, the Mulla astonished the attendants by giving each of them a gold coin as he left. When he returned the following week, the attendants were all over him, offering him massage, perfume, and expensive soap. But as he left, he gave each one a measly copper coin, saying, "This is for last time and what I gave last time was for this time." Sufi teachers say that if we open our minds and hearts to the larger picture, we shall be able to cope well with both the largesse and the losses that occur in our lives.

Likewise, awareness of the fleeting nature of time can have a very salutary effect, whether we are tempted to gloat over a temporary success or grieve over a passing sorrow. Sufis like to tell the story about a king who, having experienced many successes and failures with concomitant highs and lows in his moods, commissioned a council of the wise to create a motto that would bring him inner peace during good times and bad. The motto should remind him to restrain his exuberance during happy times and retain a sense of hope during difficult times. After much deliberation, the council brought him a ruby ring on which were inscribed four words: "This too will pass." It is said that the king was well pleased and wore the ring peacefully for the rest of his life.

 # REFLECTIONS

Consider time ... truly, human beings are in loss, except those who have faith and do righteous deeds and encourage each other in the teaching of Truth and of patient perseverance. (Qur'an 103:1–3)

Value the worth of five things before they are replaced by the other five conditions: value your youthfulness before old age arrives, value health before sickness strikes, value your wealth before you become needy, value peacefulness before hardship comes, and value life before death arrives.[1] (Hadith)

 # PRACTICE

What are your personal and spiritual goals? Make a habit of listing them on paper at least three times a year. Every time you check in, reflect on your progress.

Frame your goals in the form of prayers. Perform a ritual in which you place them in your heart, surrender them to Spirit, and ask for divine guidance. Remember to add the sentence, "This, or whatever is in my highest interest, is manifesting for me now."

The End Is Coming!

Every few years, it seems, some religious personality or another makes the news by announcing that the end of the world is nigh. Most of us just shake our heads in amusement and continue on our merry way as the Earth keeps spinning on its appointed rounds. But the Qur'an also warns us that the end is coming—though maybe not imminently—and we would be wise to pay attention. On that day, says the Qur'an, "When the sky is rent apart; when the stars are scattered; when the oceans burst forth; and when the graves are turned upside down, then shall each soul know what it has sent ahead and what it has kept back" (82:1–5). "O human being!" cries the Holy Book. "What has seduced you away from your Most Generous Instructor?" (82:6). Such is the Qur'an's dramatic description of the end times, which it variously calls the Day of Resurrection, the Day of Judgment, the Day of Great News, the Overwhelming Event, and the Day of Noise and Clamor.

Sufi teachers say these verses are intended to inspire feelings of awe and wonder about meeting the indescribable mystery of our Creator, but, sadly, unscrupulous fire-and-brimstone clerics use them to arouse fear and manipulate congregants to agree with their beliefs. The Mulla is critical of such tactics and unfazed by their depiction of irrational fear. Someone asked the Mulla, "Aren't you scared of end times?" He replied, "Which one?" "What do you mean, 'Which one'?" asked the villager. "How can there be more than one?" Replied the Mulla, "There are two: the lesser and greater end. If my wife dies before me, that is the lesser end of the world. When I die, that is the greater end of the world!"

The Mulla is particularly disapproving of people who pretend to have secret knowledge about when the end times are coming. A group of acquaintances had their eyes on his fatted lamb, so they banded together with a devious but fiery cleric to convince the Mulla that the Day of Resurrection was approaching. "In that case," they said, "we may as well celebrate grandly one last time with roasted lamb on the eve of the momentous day." The Mulla agreed to sacrifice his lamb, and on the appointed evening his guests ate heartily until the late hours of the night. Then, feeling stuffed and bloated, they fell asleep. It was a cold night, so the Mulla, being a gracious host, lit a bonfire to keep them warm. Just before dawn he awakened them to greet the Overwhelming Event, and the shivering guests clamored for their coats. "Don't worry about them," said the Mulla. "I figured you won't need them after the Resurrection, so I used them to light the fire!"

REFLECTION

They ask you about the Final Hour—when will be its appointed time? Say: "The knowledge thereof is with my Lord alone: none but He can reveal as to when it will occur." (Qur'an 7:187)

PRACTICE

What are your beliefs about end times? Do you take scriptural descriptions literally, or do you regard them as allegories and metaphors for the great mystery that lies ahead? Either way, how do your beliefs affect the way you live your life?

It's Not Like You Think It Is

In Turkey there is a puzzling tomb for the legendary Mulla. It has an impressive door with padlocks and chains—but no walls! That's not what we expect a tomb to look like, and that is precisely the Mulla's message about death and the afterlife: It almost certainly won't be whatever we may expect. Mystics say there is indeed "traffic and trade" in the mysterious realms, but that traffic and trade will remain a mystery to us until we cross to the other side at the end of our life. Trying to plumb the great beyond with our limited faculties is, the sages say, like trying to measure the depth of the ocean with a bamboo stick. It just can't be done.

But that doesn't stop us from trying, and people of all faiths have conjured up stories and allegories to deal with the hopes, fears, and curiosity we all feel about our transition from this life to whatever happens next. The truth is no one knows what happens after death.

A just king visited a holy man who was on his deathbed and made an earnest request: "When the Light has completely graced you, and you come into the nearness of Divinity, please remember me to God." To which the holy man replied, "When I step into that Presence and the Light of Splendor shines over me, I will no more even remember myself. How do you expect me to remember you?"

Some Muslim clerics give credence to a false *hadith* claiming that two fierce-looking angels named Munkar and Nakir visit the dead in their graves and ask them three specific questions about their religious beliefs. Based on the answers, the dead are either tormented or left alone to await the Day of Resurrection. The *hadith* is actually contrary to the words and spirit of the Qur'an, but the Mulla does not want to take any chances. He instructs his family to bury him in an old grave so that when the two angels come to visit, he can wave them on, saying that the grave has already been inspected!

What about the Day of Resurrection and Judgment when, according to the Qur'an, the dead will arise from their graves and be called to account for their deeds and misdeeds on Earth? The

Qur'an itself states that some of its passages are literal and others are metaphorical, and the human mind is inadequate to grasp their true meanings. No one knows if the graphic descriptions of Judgment Day are meant to be taken literally, but once again, the Mulla is unwilling to take any chances. "Don't place a headstone on my grave," he tells his family. "When I arise from my grave, I don't want my head to bang against the headstone. On the day of accountability, I want to be as clearheaded as possible."

Sufi teachers are aware of the paradox of our being questioned and judged by the All-Compassionate and All-Knowing God who, after all, created us in love and already knows our every thought and deed. These enlightened sages playfully say that they will make two requests of God: "Please plead and advocate on my behalf with Yourself" and "Do what is worthy of You and not me."

Many of us, both Christian and Muslim, grew up with frightening images of the everlasting hellfire prepared for those who stray from the path of righteousness. The Mulla knew better than to believe in such a Hell, for he once had a dream in which his wife sent him to Hell to bring back fire for her cooking, and the angel in charge told him there was no literal fire in Hell. Instead, the angel told the Mulla, people arrive in Hell fueled by their anger and hate, and that is the cause of a fire that burns within. Whether any kind of Hell actually exists or not, many spiritual leaders teach that it consists not of burning fire but of a painful separation from the glorious presence of God. Sufi teachers describe hell as a place of purification, a crucible of divine mercy where those who did not do their inner work and are smeared with the dross of negativity now have an opportunity to cleanse and refine themselves. Once they are purified, the mysterious journey continues into further realms.

Just as Qur'anic descriptions of Hell are only metaphorical, so are descriptions of Heaven. Our human hearts may delight in the image of lofty mansions, luxuriant gardens, and flowing rivers, but the Holy Book makes it clear that "the greatest bliss is the Good Pleasure of God: that is the supreme felicity" (Qur'an 9:72).

Spiritual teachers warn against living our lives based solely on the fear of Hell and desire for Heaven. Such a narrow focus deprives us of the sacred joy that we could be experiencing here and now. The famed

Imam Ghazzali tells the story of Prophet Jesus's encounters with three groups of people. The first group was physically crippled and mentally miserable. "What is your affliction?" Jesus asked. They replied, "We have become like this through our fear of Hell." The second group was similarly crippled and told Jesus, "Intense desire for Paradise has made us like this." The third group had endured much but radiated love and joy. They told Jesus, "We love the Spirit of Truth. We have glimpsed Reality, and this has made us oblivious of lesser goals."[2] May we be like the people in that third group, loving the Spirit of Truth wherever it manifests in our lives. We may have some anxieties and regrets at the end of our lives, but let us not have cause to regret, as the Mulla said, that we did not laugh enough. Instead, let us heed the wisdom of Hafiz, who says, "God wants to see more love and playfulness in your eyes, for that is your greatest witness to Him."

REFLECTIONS

O you who have faith! Be conscious of God with all the consciousness that is due Him, and do not allow death to overtake you before you have surrendered yourselves to Him. (Qur'an 3:102)

O my Lord, if I worship You from fear of Hell, burn me in Hell; and if I worship you from hope of Paradise, exclude me from Paradise. But if I worship You for Your own sake, do not withhold from me Your Eternal Beauty.[3] (Rabia)

When you were born, everyone was smiling, but you were crying. Live such a life that when you depart, everyone is weeping but you are smiling. (Hadith)

PRACTICE

Imagine that you were going to die soon. Ask yourself: What remains unsaid and to whom? What remains undone and why? Write down what you need to say and do, and prioritize the list. Then start taking care of unfinished business with humility, sincerity, and persistence. You will experience fulfillment and joyous freedom, and your fear of death will be greatly reduced.

Whenever you are anxious about how to prioritize the urgent list of things you have to do, ask yourself, "Which is closest to the Light?" Or "If I were to die soon, which one has highest priority?" Focus on that which is closest to the Light without avoiding the others. The Light, it is said, takes care of the others. Sufi masters say there is a great secret here for those who can grasp it.

Notes

Introduction
1. Idries Shah, *The Way of the Sufi* (London: Penguin Group, 1990), 178.

Our Human Condition
1. Llewellyn Vaughan-Lee, *Travelling the Path of Love: Sayings of Sufi Masters* (San Francisco: The Golden Sufi Center, 1994), 27.
2. Sherenederuz.wordpress.com/2013/04/11/2865/
3. Farid Al-Din Attar, *Muslim Saints and Mystics: Episodes from the Tadkhirat al-Auliya* (London: Penguin Group, 1966), 112.

Some Shifts in Awareness
1. Rabindranath Tagore, *Gitanjali* (Trivandrum, India: Gitanjali Press 2013), 34.
2. Inayat Khan and Coleman Barks, *The Hand of Poetry: Five Mystic Poets of Persia* (New York: Omega Publications, 1993), 23.
3. Carl Jung, *Mysterium Cuniunctionis, 1955–1956: The Collected Works of C. J. Jung*, vol. 14, trans. G. Adler and R.F.C. Hull (Princeton, NJ: Princeton University Press, 1977).

Foibles and Vulnerabilities
1. As reported by Fariduddin Attar in his thirteenth-century book *Tadkhirat al-Auliya*.
2. Al-Mamun Al-Suhrawardhy, *The Sayings of Muhammad* (London: Archibald Constable, 1905), 56, 57.
3. Robert Frager and James Fadiman, *Essential Sufism* (San Francisco: HarperCollins, 1997), 62–63.
4. Ibid., 202.
5. Idries Shah, *The Way of the Sufi* (London: Penguin Group, 1990), 102.

Wariness of Religious Institutions
1. Idries Shah, *The Way of the Sufi* (London: Penguin Group, 1990), 167.
2. Charles Kimball, *When Religion Becomes Evil: Five Warning Signs* (San Francisco: HarperOne, 2008).

Spiritual Practices
1. Idries Shah, *The Way of the Sufi* (London: Penguin Group, 1990), 136.
2. Banglaphoto.wordpress.com/category/daily-life/page/2/

Wisdom for the Inner Journey
1. Camille Helminski, *The Book of Character* (Watsonville, CA: Book Foundation, 2004), 70, 273.
2. Jane Ziegelman, *New York Times,* August 3, 2011.
3. Robert Frager and James Fadiman, *Essential Sufism* (San Francisco: HarperCollins, 1997), 63.
4. Ibid., 145.
5. Idries Shah, *The Way of the Sufi* (London: Penguin Group, 1990), 291.

Knowing God

1. Daniel Ladinsky, *The Gift* (New York: Penguin Group, 1999), 250.
2. Robert Frager and James Fadiman, *Essential Sufism* (San Francisco: HarperCollins, 1997), 200.
3. Andrew Harvey and Eryk Hanut, *Perfume of the Desert* (Wheaton, IL: Theosophical Publishing House, 1992), 41.
4. Michael Slackman, "With a Word, Egyptians Leave It All to Fate," *New York Times*, June 20, 2008.

Be Engaged in the World

1. Camille Helminski, *The Book of Character* (Watsonville, CA: Book Foundation, 2004), 101–102.
2. Robert Frager and James Fadiman, *Essential Sufism* (San Francisco: HarperCollins, 1997), 84.
3. Ibn Arabi, R.W.J. Austin, and Titus Burckhardt, *Ibn Arabi: The Bezels of Wisdom* (Mahwah, NJ: Paulist Press, 1980), 275.
4. songsofheart.wordpress.com/2012/12/18every-child-comes-with-a-message-that-god-is-not-yet-discouraged-by-man-rabindrath-tagore/

Time to Return Home

1. Robert Frager and James Fadiman, *Essential Sufism* (San Francisco: HarperCollins, 1997), 90.
2. Idries Shah, *The Way of the Sufi* (London: Penguin Group, 1990), 58.
3. Robert Frager and James Fadiman, *Essential Sufism* (San Francisco: HarperCollins, 1997), 86.

Suggestions for Further Reading

Barks, Coleman. *The Essential Rumi*. New York: HarperCollins, 1997.

Cleary, Thomas. *Living and Dying with Grace*: *Counsels of Hadrat Ali*. Boston: Shambhala, 1996.

Fadiman, James, and Robert Frager. *Essential Sufism*. San Francisco: HarperCollins, 1997.

Helminski, Camille. *The Book of Character*: *Writings on Character and Virtue from Islamic and Other Sources*. Watsonville, CA: The Book Foundation, 2004.

Helminski, Camille, and Kabir Helminski. *Jewels of Remembrance*: *A Daybook of Spiritual Guidance Containing 365 Selections from the Wisdom of Mevlana Jalaluddin Rumi*. Putney, VT: Threshold Books, 1996.

———. *Rumi: Daylight—A Daybook of Spiritual Guidance*. Boston: Shambhala, 1999.

Houston, Jean. *The Search for the Beloved*: *Journeys in Mythology and Sacred Psychology*. New York: Tarcher, 1997.

Ladinsky, Daniel. *The Gift*: *Poems by Hafiz, the Great Sufi Master*. New York: Penguin, 1999.

———. *Love Poems from God*: *Twelve Sacred Voices from the East and West*. New York: Penguin, 2002.

Llewellyn, Vaughan-Lee. *Sufism*: *The Transformation of the Heart*. San Francisco: The Golden Sufi Center, 1995.

———. *Travelling the Path of Love*: *Sayings of Sufi Masters*. San Francisco: The Golden Sufi Center, 1995.

Rahman, Jamal. *The Fragrance of Faith*: *The Enlightened Heart of Islam*. Watsonville, CA: The Book Foundation, 2004.

———. *Spiritual Gems of Islam*: *Insights and Practices from the Qur'an, Hadith, Rumi, and Muslim Teaching Stories to Enlighten the Heart and Mind*. Woodstock, VT: SkyLight Paths Publishing, 2013.

Rahman, Jamal, Kathleen Schmit Elias, and Ann Holmes Redding. *Out of Darkness into Light*: *Spiritual Guidance in the Qur'an with Reflections from Jewish and Christian Scriptures*. New York: Morehouse, 2009.

Shah, Idries. *The Exploits of the Incomparable Mulla Nasruddin*. London: The Octagon Press, 1983.

———. *The Pleasantries of the Incredible Mulla Nasruddin*. New York: E. P. Dutton and Company, 1971.

———. *The Subtleties of the Inimitable Mulla Nasruddin*. London: The Octagon Press, 1983.

———. *The Way of the Sufi*. London: Penguin Group, 1990.

Starr, Mirabai. *God of Love*: *A Guide to the Heart of Judaism, Christianity, and Islam*. Rhinebeck, NY: Monkfish, 2012.

Sis, Peter. *The Conference of the Birds*. New York: Penguin, 2011.

About SKYLIGHT PATHS Publishing

SkyLight Paths Publishing is creating a place where people of different spiritual traditions come together for challenge and inspiration, a place where we can help each other understand the mystery that lies at the heart of our existence.

Through spirituality, our religious beliefs are increasingly becoming a part of our lives—rather than *apart* from our lives. While many of us may be more interested than ever in spiritual growth, we may be less firmly planted in traditional religion. Yet, we do want to deepen our relationship to the sacred, to learn from our own as well as from other faith traditions, and to practice in new ways.

SkyLight Paths sees both believers and seekers as a community that increasingly transcends traditional boundaries of religion and denomination—people wanting to learn from each other, *walking together, finding the way.*

For your information and convenience, at the back of this book we have provided a list of other SkyLight Paths books you might find interesting and useful. They cover the following subjects:

Buddhism / Zen	Global Spiritual	Monasticism
Catholicism	Perspectives	Mysticism
Children's Books	Gnosticism	Poetry
Christianity	Hinduism /	Prayer
Comparative	Vedanta	Religious Etiquette
Religion	Inspiration	Retirement
Current Events	Islam / Sufism	Spiritual Biography
Earth-Based	Judaism	Spiritual Direction
Spirituality	Kabbalah	Spirituality
Enneagram	Meditation	Women's Interest
	Midrash Fiction	Worship

Printed in the USA
CPSIA information can be obtained
at www.ICGtesting.com
JSHW082337140824
68134JS00020B/1734

9 781594 735479